TOTALITARIAN
TRIALS

An Essay

BY
CISCO MARTO

outskirts
press

Table of Contents

Prologue

The *Politics of Aristotle,* a philosophical work from 400 BC had a profound influence on posterity. In ancient Athens, the capital of Greek culture, while attending the Academy of Plato, Aristotle taught that the state is a creature of nature and that man is by nature a political animal. Man is a unique being endowed with the gift of speech and fully capable to reason between good and evil. Aristotle's first book of politics is about the countless apathetic people who think politics and government issues are irrelevant matters for others to resolve. When in reality they are a direct path to securing the basic creature needs of the family, community and village or what Aristotle called "the good life." And to live this kind of life, a person must be free to determine his or her own ends and have the wherewithal to have a realistic chance of achieving those ends.

Aristotle's second book on politics revolts against the Communist strain in Plato's *Republic.* Aristotle discloses, "Plato is my friend but the truth is my friend even more." And he scorns Plato's illogical concept of ending family life and abolishing private properties in favor of an elite, centralized communistic society.

Aristotle points out that wealth is desirable, not as an ends in itself, but as a means to ensure social stability. After engaging in debate and classic arguments on the subject, Aristotle's preference always settled on a constitutional form of government in which power lies with the responsible property-owning members of society. He further advised that the Utopian communistic government contrived by Plato is a self-destructive concept that never will work. As predicted, Plato's convoluted communist theory went unheeded for a millennium, never to reemerge until the Age of Exploration when European voyagers first colonized the new world of America.

The School of Athens / Raphael / Fresco, 1509 and 1511
Eric Vandeville / akg-images

CHAPTER 1

Virginia Company of London 1607

Seventeenth Century England was rife with religious bigotry, political instability and financial pandemonium. The English Reformation of King Henry VIII's legacy willed a despotic government. His ruin was six dismissive marriages two of his wives were guillotined after which he refuted the authority of the Catholic Pope and then dared to declare himself head of the Church of England. Religious bigotry between the Anglicans and separatist Puritans, along with socioeconomic problems ensued. Upon the kings death, his daughter inherited the throne, and gained fame as the Virgin Queen Elizabeth I. She reigned with absolute authority keeping a tight rein on expenditures due to heavy government debt and critical grain and food shortages. The resolute queen often encouraged sea voyages to the unexplored North American Coast but her shrewdness was suspect as food was scarce and vagabonds slept in the streets of London. Queen Elizabeth I, never to wed, remained the sole monarch of England for over four decades. She died in 1603. The reigning King James VI of Scotland inherited the English throne along with Ireland; he united the crowns and proclaimed his joint kingdom of Great Britain.

In the midst of political turmoil there emerged a group of wealthy speculators known as the Virginia Company of London. They crafted a daring public offer in their search for adventurers brave enough to set sail for fame and fortune in the New World. It all came to pass on December 20, 1606. On a frigid morning in London three tall ships manned by a 144 courageous men, weighed anchor, and set sail on a gallant adventure. The three tiered wooden ships overladen with supplies navigated unheeded up the Thames River. Sooner than could be imagined, their high-spirited cruise turned into a voyage of grim peril and misery. Lives were lost to an unyielding ocean during four punishing months of fighting off hunger, scurvy, and the blustery winter winds of the North Atlantic. Their long, perilous voyage looked hopeless till April 1607.

Twas an early morning fog that blanked the eastern coast of North America. The three weather-beaten ships drifted in the doldrums of a dead calm sea. Wind starved sails hung limp in a dense fog that held back the dawn. All aboard the battered ships were either asleep or lifeless. The deathlike silence was shattered by a loud mouthed sailor aloft in in the crow's nest. "Ahoy, ahoy below," he bellowed. "Seagulls aloft, Captain. No shore in sight." Confusion broke out below deck. Cries of joy filled the air as sunlight filters through the morning mist. All eyes focused on rolling white caps breaking up in shallow waters and, there looming large on the horizon--- **land, dead ahead!**

Susan Constant Ship
1607
Joseph Sohm / Shutter Stock

Standing tall at the ship's helm was one of England's finest command-ers. A one-armed sea master was he: Captain Christopher Newport. All of a sudden: he whirled the ship wheel hard left. His aim was to move on for another forty miles upstream in search of a safe, deep wa-ter harbor in Chesapeake Bay. He managed to anchored his 116-foot flagship, the Susan Constant, in safe tide waters, protected on three sides by fresh water rivers. Soon after, the "Godspeed" arrived, fol-lowed by the "Discovery" a bantam-sized supply ship. After dropping anchor one hundred stalwart sea mates carefully disembarked into small oar boats and rowed straight for the land of their dreams. Once inland they discovered crystal clear streams teeming with edible fish.

And within shouting distance, wild game roamed unruffled in the shadows of a towering forest. No other life was apparent, but concealed deep in the vast forest were wary native Indians.

Wild berries, chestnuts, strawberries and all kinds of plant life seemed to abound everywhere. The rich black earth underfoot was fertile, a soil well suited for farming. The weary voyagers were dumbfounded at the sight of it all. The faithful among them mouthed silent prayers of gratitude while many a jaundiced eyes peered long and hard, trying to distinguish reality from delusion. This was the very moment of truth for the brave voyagers who were awed by the sheer bounty of it all. A land of plenty and it was theirs for the picking--- being the first settlers in this corner of North America.

Without any further delay, a handmade wooden cross was ceremoniously erected by the group. All in unison dropped to their knees to thank God for deliverance to a land of plenty. Being duly authorized by the "Virginia Company of London," they went forward to found an Anglo-American colony; and declared that this site in the New World; henceforth would be known as **Jamestown...** in honor of King James I of England.

Rules of Colonization....

Deliberately held in abeyance until this critical point--- Captain Christopher Newport revealed that he had the all-important rules of colonization issued by the Royal Council of London. He opened a sealed manuscript and read aloud the predetermined names of seven men duly authorized to be the councilors and work supervisors for the First Company in Virginia. The president of the council was Edward M. Wingfield. Four others, all former army officers, and two of the ship captains would be in charge of groups of colonist, with the exception of the seventh man named. He was a mercenary arrested aboard ship by Captain Newport for inciting a mutiny. The fabled prisoner was none other than John Smith. Contrary to future history books, he was jailed and withheld from the council. He managed to avoid criminal charges for mutiny but later was charged for other serious offenses of gross negligence and sentenced under Levitical law to be hanged. John Smith managed to escape the gallows in Virginia, sailed back home--- only to conceal his guilt and spin the truth of the matter into a fictitious story.

This being the first charter of colonization in the 1600's, the rights of the heroic settlers were supposed to be guaranteed, but unfortunately these men were given absolutely no voice in the government of Jamestown. The Virginia Company of London's charter was incorporated in the midst of total political confusion and economic failure. As fate would have it, famed Englishman; Sir Thomas More's sixteenth century political book "Utopia," was heralded and in vogue with Britons, and thought to be a paradigm of peace and security. Thomas More's political utopia, when fused with Plato's communistic ideas in the "*Republic*," appeared to be a credible political concept. The rest is history. The Virginia Company of London Council authorized this as a governmental trial for the first colony of North America.

Regrettably; Jamestown leaders found themselves contract bound to enforce a strict communal society compelling all settlers to perform collective labor and to put their harvests in a common storehouse for all to share equally. Private property was never to be allowed. Ironically all the brave voyagers were resolute refugees; at great personal risk they had fled their homeland in search of liberty and social freedom.... Instead, without warning, they were being used as indentured slaves, laboring as physical surrogates for an embryonic communist society. Totalitarian regulations proved to be counter-productive and unprofitable. Many individuals refused to work harder for the sake of their lazy or unproductive fellow workers, only to share the rewards equally with the slackers. There's was a hopeless existence not to be questioned, only to do or die. Twice a day the men were marched into the fields to the beat of a drum. Never to be rewarded with a living wage or any personal reward inevitably resulted in poor crops which inevitably lead to starvation. Within six months, by early spring only thirty-eight able-bodied men were still alive. Many died of scurvy and respiratory disease, but most suffered a slow, painful death by starvation during the first winter.

The surviving assemblage of bony colonists were saved. A shipload of five hundred additional settlers armed with fresh supplies sailed into Jamestown in 1609. Unfortunately misery, suffering, and depravity rose up again. This time the starvation and hostilities were even greater and deadlier. Four hundred and forty of the new arrivals tried their best, but they too died within six months. Back in London; the elitist Royal Council, which was in denial, questioned; how so many people could possibly starve to death when there was an abundance of meat, fish and fruits. Jamestown supervisors and the haggard colonist's knew damn well the reasons why and ever so candidly spelled out the cruel truth for their elitist masters: ***"The fault was not in the bareness and defect of the country, but in the want of providence, industry, and need of better government."***

The Governor of Jamestown grudgingly complied within the dogmatic rules of the communistic charter; death became rampant, the entire settlement was doomed. Only then, out of sheer desperation, private property in the form of land ownership was offered as a last-ditch effort before the agony of mass burials. It was Deputy Governor, Sir Thomas Dale who trashed the contracted totalitarian rules, without any further consent, he abandoned the concept of communal agriculture and collectivism. Every still surviving family or individual was given a three acre parcel of land to farm to feed their own family and told to plant and grow their own crops to the best of their ability. Henceforth, to each his own.

It worked. Miraculously the survivors lived on and multiplied by producing ample quantities of corn, beans, lettuce, squash, tobacco, and other crops. The remedy, personal ownership of land, meant no more indentured servitude. It also was the means for proud property owners to thrive and sustain themselves as self-sufficient human beings and to live virtuous lives in accordance with Divine Providence. The people found a better form of government. It was about soul and freedom, democratic individualism and newborn free markets.

The liberated colonists' endowment continued to grow, and eventually all the land and property in Jamestown was converted to private ownership. The growing population needed and built a church, hundreds of thatched houses, general trading stores, and a huge central storehouse for the new tobacco trading company. Tobacco suddenly was in great demand in London. John Rolfe, a local settler developed his own hybrid seeds which became Jamestown first exported cash crop. Within ten years plantations extended twenty miles along the James River. Back in England merchants purchased assorted commodities and merchandise from other parts of the world in order to trade for many boatloads of premium hybrid tobacco from the Colonial Jamestown Company.

The sudden global exchange of goods and wealth gave birth to free-market capitalism and the exchange of all kinds of goods. The potential cash value of tobacco crops soared incredibly. By 1622, the Colonies tobacco actually became a valued currency that was broadly used as money, valuable enough to exchange for solid Gold.

Jamestown officially became an English Crown Colony in 1624 and celebrated with the arrival of another five thousand free-trading English capitalists.

CHAPTER 2

The Plymouth Company 1620

British colonization caught on with news of a Crown Colony called Jamestown, Virginia, located in North America. Political bedlam and religious bigotry prevailed across Europe. The idea of living in the New World of America was a dream for many; it was a land of religious and social freedom, and real independence. There were also enterprising business-men with uncommitted venture capital in search of foreign trade and commerce

A second charter was unanimously approved by the Council of New England. The *Mayflower,* an aged English merchant ship, sailed out of Plymouth, England in August. On board the three- masted vessel were 102 high-spirited passengers bound for a new life in Jamestown, Virginia. The North Atlantic crossing proved to be horrendous. The Mayflower, being a small three-tier timber ship, was awash by tower-ing waves in a nor'easter storm that wrecked the stern and rudder. The ship stayed afloat but was blown far off course during raging gales. Two passengers died. All aboard believed they were hopelessly lost at sea. The weather-beaten ship wandered aimlessly for weeks before land was sighted in November 1620. They made landfall alright but unfortunately found themselves moored five hundred miles north of their destination the Jamestown Colony.

Where-ever they were, all knew that they had to stay put; if they were to survive. It was near Cape Cod that their leader, William Bradford rowed his congregation of religious separatists (pilgrims) to the rocky shores. The pious congregated huddled together in solemn prayer, thanking God Almighty for his mercy and delivery to the New World. All agreed their greatest want was simply to live, work, and pray right there, free of religious persecution. They were just peace-loving, hardworking members of what they liked to call their own Plymouth Plantation.

The Pilgrims had a reputation for virtue, ambition, and productivity. They were undaunted by alleged rumors of short-comings by the Virginia Company. Knowing that, they still willingly agreed to accept the company rules of a communal livelihood, which meant collectivization of crops; and once again, no private property ownership. Unfortunately; **history was to about to repeat itself with the Plymouth Company.** Once more; there were many able bodied men who worked very hard, but also there were others who didn't. And tragically a shared livelihood depends on the cooperative effort of everyone or the commune collapses.

The fate of the Plymouth Company communal trial once again proved to be disastrous. Communistic governance bred confusion and dissension. With few supplies and poor crops, famine ensued and disease spread. After just four months of winter weather only half of the original 102 settlers were still alive by April, 1621. Devastated by the calamity, and no way to halt the misery, William Bradford, signor of the "*Mayflower Compact*," and governor of Plymouth Colony, sent a caustic letter to his directors, the financial backers in London. No words were wasted nor apology engendered, but in complete candor he wrote. "***Let none argue that this is due to human failing, rather than this is due to this communistic plan of life itself. I answer,*** *seeing that all men have this feeling in them, that God in his wisdom saw another plan of life fitter for them."*

Governor Bradford being a man of virtue, pledged to save the suffering Pilgrims from this pagan trial of communism. Being out of reach of his English masters, Bradford defiantly ended communal property and labor; instead he reverted to private ownership of property by setting aside land for each individual to own and cultivate. His challenge was quite plain-spoken: *"If a man will not work, he shall not eat."* There were no regrets or any hesitations.

Exuberant Pilgrims praised the Lord for their share of earth gracefully bestowed to their trust. To Governor William Bradford they were forever beholden, for ending the deadly tenets of communism. By granting the settlers rational incentives, Governor Bradford essentially not only improved personal well being but also totally enriched their quality of life. The upshot was absolutely amazing. Bountiful crops put an end to the relentless famine and energized the colony back to life. The autumn harvest of 1623, found colonists and native Indians feasting together; three days of Thanksgiving festivities celebrated the plethora of food and new-found liberties. Private property ownership proved to be a path to prosperity. These brave-hearts set the course of destiny. They cast the first fertile seeds of liberty, religious freedom, and free markets that could and would flourish for future generations of Americans.

As early as 1641, the local son of a Puritan minister and resident lawyer drafted a document establishing colonial rights even though they were still under the British Crown. It was a statement of principles for governance that provided for one hundred individual liberties. The General Court established the hundred laws which were called the *"Massachusetts Body of Liberties."* The document established the basic principles of sacredness of life, liberty, and property and stipulated rules for judicial proceedings. The colonies continued to prosper and the population grew by leaps and bounds. By the 1700's, more than a million industrious colonists had settled in the New World.

The early American settlements of Jamestown and Plymouth sustained colonization with an upsurge rush of extraordinary pioneers who paved the way for better methods of commerce. After the failed Communist trial of collectivism and communal living clarified the critical need to establish ethical form of capitalism. Here was a pilot program for future American economic systems based on private property and a free market that offered political and social freedom. During the ensuing years, the introduction of modern democracy with a unique capitalist free enterprise system gave rise to modern commerce in the New World of America at a time when many countries still lived under a feudal system.

A minor faction of Eastern European socialists, then as now, argued that the capitalistic societies of the colonies were in constant discord. The Socialists calculated role was to manipulate and radically change public opinion, disrupt existing social order, and abolish all capitalism. Fortunately their firebrand of ideology remained dormant for centuries; in wait of a malleable government in peril.

CHAPTER 3

New World Democracy

The year was 1831. A French nobleman charted a mission of foreign intrigue for himself. Alexis de Tocqueville, a distinguished sociologist, lawyer, and historian extraordinaire sought the social merit and character of a working democracy found only in early America. While living in Paris, he endured the fury of the French Revolution. Early on, both of his parents were imprisoned during a reign of terror. He had witnessed raging anarchists running wild though the streets of the city. Smoking cannons and rapid gunfire failed to halt the mobs of charging protesters all screaming, "A la guillotine." It was during the bloody summer rebellion in 1830 when Parisians cried and died for a new constitutional monarchy. Alexis de Tocqueville was convinced that a collapse of French aristocracy was imminent. By August, King Charles X abdicated the throne, and fled with his son to England. The scale of the revolution convinced Tocqueville that the provincial France of old was moving toward a democracy and the New World democracy found in America would be a worthy case study and possibly good for the future stability of France.

Alexis de Tocqueville and company set sail out of Le Havre, France, in April 1831 his destination was the state of New York in America. The crossing was miserable to say the least. After thirty- seven treacherous days and nights, covering three thousand miles of rolling seas, with the gale force winds of the North Atlantic, the weather-worn ship dropped anchor in the port city of Newport, Rhode Island. From there Tocqueville traveled overland to New York City. For the next nine months he journeyed far and wide over majestic mountain ranges, mighty rivers, and seven thousand miles of furrowed dirt pathways. He traveled by stagecoach to Philadelphia and on horseback to Baltimore and Boston. The Frenchman was well received in Washington DC. by President, Andrew Jackson, John Quincy Adams, and the chief justice of the Supreme Court. After enjoying a successful meeting in Washington, he traveled northward to Green Bay, Wisconsin, and the great north-west woods. He continued north to the Canadian border before turning south by southwest aboard a flatboat all the way down the Mississippi River to New Orleans and the Gulf of Mexico.

Alexis de Tocqueville chronicled the following for historians: "Those coasts, so admirably adapted for commerce and industry; those wide and deep rivers; that valley of the Mississippi; the whole continent in short, seemed prepared to be the abode of **a great nation yet unborn.** The United States of America has only been emancipated for half a century from the state of colonial dependence in which it stood up to Great Britain; the number of large fortunes there is small, and capital is still scarce. Yet no people in the world have made such rapid progress in trade and manufactures as the Americans; they constitute at the present day the second maritime nation in the world."

"It had stood the test of time and trial of many hardships but proved to be a government of liberty regulated by law. Nothing, in my opinion, is more deserving of our attention than the intellectual and moral associations of America. They owe nothing to any man, they expect nothing from any man; they acquire the habit of always considering themselves as standing alone, and they are apt to imagine that their whole destiny is in their own hands. That sort of intellectual freedom which equality may give ought, therefore, to be very carefully distinguished from anarchy which revolution brings. There are no revolutions."

"It must never be forgotten that religion gave birth to Anglo-American society.

In the United States, religion is therefore mingled with all the habits of the nation and all the feelings of patriotism, whence it derives a peculiar force. In America religion has, as it were, laid down its own limits. Religious institutions have remained wholly distinct from political institutions. There is, and I cannot repeat it too often, there is here matter for profound reflection to those who look on freedom of thought as a holy thing and who hate not only the despot, but despotism. The Americans having admitted the principal doctrines of the Christian religion without inquiry are obliged to accept in like manner a great number of moral truths originating in it and connected with it. I am inclined to believe this practice of American courts to be at once the most favorable to liberty as well as to public order."

"Another circumstance to which I have alluded is that the social condition and the constitution of the Americans are democratic, but they have not had a democratic revolution. In France the constitution is immutable. In England, the Parliament has an acknowledged right to modify the constitution. **The political theories of America are simpler and more rational.** An American constitution is not supposed to be immutable as in France, nor is susceptible of modification by the ordinary powers of society as in England. But it is better to grant the power of changing the constitution of the people to men who represent (however imperfectly) the will of the people, rather than to men who represent no one but themselves. In America the constitution may therefore vary, but as long as it exists it is the origin of all authority, and sole vehicle of the predominating force. It is perfectly natural that in a free country like America all should have the right of indicting public functionaries before the ordinary tribunals."

While Alexis de Tocqueville crisscrossed America, political agitators and social scoundrels who inflamed the revolution in France had propelled a ground swell of anarchy. The stability of many governments in Europe began to crumble. The rebellion that started in Paris produced a wave of uprisings in Belgium, Italy, Greece, Poland and Tsarists Russia. Anarchists berated conservative kings and governments; even liberal groups joined with rebels rioting across the continent. Reactionaries with deep-seated ambitions for self-governing, set off widespread demonstrations of nationalism, only to be intensified by a growing catalog of conflicting ideologies.

It became a veritable battle of isms--- liberalism, republicanism, radicalism, and communism. The search for a stable form of government became imperative. Mayhem reigned supreme with a profusion of self-styled political philosophers offering many hypothetical ideologies. The Owenites in England and the Fourierists in France opposed the Chartists and the reformists. Uprisings across Germany and Prussia raged on all the while Alexis de Tocqueville was overseas collecting pertinent facts for his case study of an actual working democracy ---as in America.

German political philosopher Georg Wilhelm Friedrich Hegel, who initiated his own particular proposition called the "Hegelian Dialectic," died suddenly in 1831. Karl Marx personally grieved over Hegel's death. He was a former student. Marx was Hegel's most ardent disciple before befriending another fellow radical, Frederick Engels. Engels happened to be a supporter of Ludwig Feuerbach, who also was a former student of Hegel. It was Engels who introduced Marx to Feuerbach, a resolute atheist and author of the philosophical "Materialism." Marx and Engels saw it as a golden opportunity to seize and combine his ideology with others. They used the hypothesis of Feuerbach's material and nonspiritual ideas, and then added Hegel's dialectic philosophy as an innovative concept that could lend credibility and jump-start their own special concept of socialistic communism. The end result was that their small Socialist groups gained needed attention and momentum. Their first and foremost objective was to develop and nurture a narcissistic agenda to disrupt much of the social and political order of the time. Karl Marx, with Fredrick Engels, further combined the socialistic ideas of Robert Owen, Charles Fournier, Georg Hegel, and Ludwig Feuerbach with their own communist dogma. Subsequently, Marx and Engels finished their contemporary concept of how socialistic communism should work and had the good fortune to find a compliant publisher in London, England. Their work, **"The Communist Manifesto"** was an unproven synthesis of political ideas intended to achieve a utopian form of government. The finished product "begs the question"; in other words, it remains an illogical fallacy, in which the premise is supposed to be true, but without evidence other than their claim for it to be so. Their conclusion is based on a convoluted purpose never to be achieved in the real world--- similar to another common fallacy, "Might makes right".

On the contrary, Alexis De Tocqueville acknowledged that in America; "There was no philosophical school of their own, and they cared not for various schools of political thought." "They shared a common philosophy to accept tradition only as a means of information, and existing facts to do better; to seek the reason of things for one self was their only philosophy. The Americans combine the notions of Christianity and of liberty so intimately in their minds that it is impossible to make them conceive the one without the other."

The pseudo-intellectual European methods of collecting hypothetical theories by Socialists for the reformation of failed governments were judged futile. "American democracy" was a painstaking fact-finding mission, scientifically researched by the Frenchmen. Alexis de Tocqueville's work amounted to a study in contrasts. His fact finding mission necessitated traveling across America to small towns and crowded cities, greeting and interviewing farmers, bankers, hundreds of common folks, teachers, and politicians of consequence, always careful to document his critical analysis of an actual thriving democracy. His findings and conclusions were heralded as a masterful political critique. "Democracy of America" was published on Tocqueville's return to France. The first edition in 1835 sold out worldwide, as did the second edition and all that followed during the next century. In 1837, he was named to the Legion of Honor for his book.

Whenever asked, "Socialism or democracy?" Alexis de Tocqueville faithfully responded:

"Socialism presents an irreconcilable conflict with Democracy. Democracy extends the sphere of individual freedom, socialism restricts it. Democracy attaches all possible value to each man; socialism makes each man a mere agent, a mere number. Democracy and Socialism have nothing in common but one word, equality. But notice the difference; while Democracy seeks equality in liberty, Socialism seeks equality in restraint and servitude."

(Excerpts from *Democracy in America*)
By Alexis De Tocqueville

Portrait of Alex Tocqueville / A. L. Noel / Lithograph, 1884
akg-images

CHAPTER 4

The Communist Manifesto Legacy

"The history of all hitherto existing society is the history of class struggles." The very first statement of Karl Marx's Manifesto, written in 1848, lacks credibility. Such an absurdity to reduce all of human existence to a single principal of economics. The truth of the matter is that common land ownership existed in Russia. Georg Ludwig von Mauer, a German statesman and legal historian, categorically proved that in fact it previously had been the social foundation from which all ancient Teutonic races started in history. By 1884, a year after Marx died. Frederick Engels was obliged to publish a new book, this time focused on the early human history following the disintegration of primitive communities and the emergence of a class society based on private property. There were subsequent edition revisions about private land ownership in 1890 and 1894.

For years on end, *proletarians* (the lower class) rarely read books of political philosophy, and the *bourgeoisie* (capitalists) had little or no use for Karl Marx's communistic writings. Meager sales relegated it to obscurity. Their term bourgeoisie refers to a class of modern capitalists, owners with means of social production and employers of wage-laborers. *Proletarians* were a class of modern wage-laborers having no means of production of their own, consequently they were reduced to physical labor in order to live.

Karl Marx did not mince words when writing the following rancor about America:

"The discovery of America, the rounding of the Cape, opened up fresh ground for the rising bourgeoisie. The East-Indian and the Chinese markets, the colonization of America, trade with the colonies, the increase in the means of exchange and in commodities, generally, gave to commerce, to navigation, to industry, an impulse never before known, and thereby, to the revolutionary element in the tottering feudal society, a rapid development. Thereupon, steam and machinery revolutionized industrial production. The place of manufacture was taken by the giant. Modern industry has established the world market for which the discovery of America paved the way. This market has given an immense development to commerce, to navigation, to communication by land. The bourgeoisie, during its rule of scarce one hundred years, has created more massive and more colossal productive forces than all preceding generations together."

No argument up to this point, but Marx surely had other Utopian ideas in mind.

The discovery and colonization of America in the seventeenth century gave rise to new methods of commerce. The deployment of foreign trade and increased productivity were milestone events that proved highly profitable but that in itself was despicable according to Karl Marx. He proceeded to denounce America's achievements as total social decadence and evil. Then he offered, as if it were his own bright idea. A politicized version of Hegel's philosophical "dialectical materialistic" theory, using it to heighten his own implausible socioeconomic concept of socialist communism.

Karl Marx and Friedrich Engels cynically presented a far-fetched spectrum of class warfare forced upon victimized proletarians when they wrote the following:

"The bourgeoisie has left remaining no other nexus between man and man than naked self-interest, than callous cash payment. It has resolved personal worth into exchange value, and in place of the number-less indefeasible chartered freedoms, has set up that single, unconscionable freedom ---Free Trade. In one word, for exploitation, veiled by religious and political illusions, it has substituted naked shameless, direct, brutal exploitation."

"The bourgeoisie has stripped of its halo every occupation hitherto honored and looked up to with reverent awe. It has converted the physician, the lawyer, the priest, the poet, the man of science, into its paid wage-laborers. A society that has conjured up such gigantic means of production and of exchange is like the sorcerer, who is no longer able to control the powers of the nether world that he has called up by his spells. **The bourgeois clap-trap about the family and education, about the hallowed co-relation of parent and child, becomes all the more disgusting, the more, by the action of Modern Industry.** The supremacy of the proletariat will cause them to vanish still faster. United action, of the leading civilized countries at least, is one of the first conditions for the emancipation of the proletariat.

In place of the old bourgeois society, with its class antagonisms, we shall have an association, in which the free development of each is the condition for the free development of all. **This cannot be affected except by means of despotic inroads on the rights of property, and on the conditions of bourgeois production by means of measures. These measures will of course will be different."**

The following measures will be applicable:

1. **Abolition of property in land** and application of all rents of land to public purposes.
2. **A heavy progressive or graduated income tax.**
3. **Abolition of all right of inheritance.**
4. **Confiscation of the property of all emigrants and rebels.**
5. **Centralization of credits in the hands of the State by means of a national bank with an exclusive monopoly.**
6. **Centralization of the means of communication and transport in the hands of the State.**
7. **Extension of factories and instruments of production owned by the State.**
8. **Equal liability of all to labor. Establishment of industrial armies, and for agriculture.**
9. **Combination of agriculture with manufacturing industries. Abolition of town borders.**
10. **Free government education for all children...** for industrial production etc., etc.

When in the course of development, class distinctions have disappeared, and all production, has been concentrated in the hands of a vast association of the whole nation the public power will lose its political character. Political power, properly so called, is merely the organized power of one class for suppressing another. In place of the old bourgeois society, with its classes and class antagonisms, we shall have an association, in which the free development of each is the condition for the free development of all. **(Marx and Engels literary work, 1850)**

The "Communist Manifesto" is not a profound political treatise but rather a deceptive scheme for gaining power--- absolute power in a classless society. Simple logic, as well as history, dictates that a government will always establish a separate social class--- the ruling class. If and when, a Socialist revolution routs the evil (bourgeoisie) or capitalists, **the only classes remaining, would be the (powerful) rulers and the non-rulers (no political power)**. In turn, the powerful elite ruler's looming plan will be to abolish private property with collective control of all means of production, while the non-rulers will live at best; **"from each according to his ability, to each according to their needs."** Marx's pitiful knowledge of economics fails to figure or even detail productivity into his Utopian scheme other than his contrarian effects to undermine it.

As for the ancient Greek noun dialectic, it originally meant no more than a method of study or argument employed by Socrates while in dialogue with associates. His unique process was to begin with a question about the nature of something, and proceed to lengthy discussions of various assumptions before arriving at a reasonable conclusion. The word dialectic was redefined by Hegel. The art of arriving at the truth by disclosing contradictions became an applied political process called the Hegelian dialectic. Marx arrogantly expanded on his mentor's basic concept by presenting mandatory conflicts designed to guide mankind into social utopia. The theory was that there is no absolute truth anywhere, but "truth" is to be found in **synthesis**, as a result of compromise of the **thesis** (position), contested against an **antithesis** (contradictory/position). This is the essence of the dialectic process. Unfortunately no matter what the thesis may be, the covert dialectic aims to control both the conflict, and the resolution of differences, which subsequently **leads everyone involved into a new and greater cycle of conflict.**

Materialism, the philosophical concept of Ludwig Feuerbach encouraged mind over matter. He argues that all of nature is matter only. His primary work consisted of the dissolution of a religious world into a secular one. He regarded religion as the enemy of all progress; freed from religious restraints people will materialistically change the world via revolutions. Marx seized upon Feuerbach's atheistic viewpoint as a good fit with Hegel's dialectic concept; the contrarian interactions of both would produce a synthesis and when Marx's dialectical materialism was applied to the history of social development it would no doubt generate a revolutionary thrust of social changes.

This convoluted theory simply justifies conflict and endless war.

Marx imagined himself a political mastermind who brilliantly discovered the missing key to human history. His doctrine was purposely fixed upon the revolutionary overthrow of inferior existing social systems and, religious orthodoxy, along with the abolition of private property. Marx continued to fuse Hegelian dialectics and materialism into a composite as his basic proof that Utopian socialism (communism) was certain to reign "with the inexorability of the law of nature."

There was in fact never any real, functional Socialist economics. Last but not least, no alternative or course of action was ever offered; if in the event there ever was some sort of mythical Utopian society. But then, it never really has been necessary because no credible synthesis was realized. The Manifesto's authors unwittingly revealed why it is all so illogical. **Of course when you abolish religious moral standards and further; "abolish eternal truths in contradiction to all past historical experience". There really can't be any such thing as logical relevance.**

Note:
The Communist Manifesto has the dubious distinction of being the ultimate rule book employed by a core of maniacal tyrants during the twentieth century.

CHAPTER 5

Karl Marx
1818 – 1883

Karl Heinrich Marx was born into a large middle-class family in Trier, Prussia, in 1818. He was a feisty youth with an attitude when he began studies at the University of Bonn, at best an average student, but in truth a rebel without a cause. During his freshman year, he was jailed for drunkenness, fell deeply in debt and barely survived a dangerous gun duel. His father Heinrich, a prominent and highly respected Jewish lawyer, was ashamed of his eldest son's disgraceful behavior and demanded that he transfer to the more sedate University of Berlin.

While studying in Berlin, young Karl became enthralled with an abstract political philosophy, known as "dialectical thinking" presented by his professor Georg Wilhelm Friedrich Hegel. He found his personal cause and joined an activist group of students involved in a movement they claimed was German idealism. All were highly critical of other people's religious and political beliefs. Karl's newly acquired radicalism further distressed his father. In a series of letters, Heinrich expressed disgust and fear that his son's demons and growing irresponsibility would be the end of him. Much to his surprise his son Karl managed to survive it all and graduated from the University of Jena in 1841. Unfortunately his persona and radical political beliefs kept him from finding employment in the field of education or for that matter, any kind of teaching position.

Frustrated, Marx decided to make a career for himself in journalism. After another full year of rejections, he was hired by the *Rheinische Zeitung*, a Socialist newspaper in Cologne, Germany. Before years end, German authorities took drastic legal action against the newspaper. Karl Marx quit his job abruptly and fled to Paris, France. While safe and sound in Paris, and after some serious soul-searching, he believed it would be best to publish on his own a far-reaching journal called "Deutsch-Franzosishe Jahrbucher," a German/French composition. This time his characteristic antisocial-political writing, which advocated "merciless criticism of everything existing," was good for only one issue. Ultimately his only real accomplishment in Paris was finding himself a new friend. Friedrich Engels, the son of a wealthy cotton manufacturer, who just happened to be a fellow contrarian political ideologue... his kind of friend. And best of all, he became Karl Marx's life-long benefactor.

Forever the fiery social critic, Marx tried once more to sell his utopian socialism, this time with the "Vorwaerts," a German newspaper based in Paris. This tabloid was his forte, more or less an instrument of a secret utopian Socialist society. Karl Marx finally gained name recognition and notoriety; but unfortunately only as a dangerous revolutionary. He was again apprehended **and permanently banished from France in 1845**.

In desperation Marx sought political asylum in Brussels, Belgium. Although this was one of the more liberal countries in Europe, authorities warned him not to publish any politically volatile books. Therefore, Marx spent his time promoting Hegel's dialectical philosophy among his network of Socialist associates in Germany, France, and England. At long last he did acquire a degree of fame among several underground politicos. An extremist group in London begged that he and his associate Friedrich Engels organize their ideas into a practical party program for formal presentation to members of their new "Communist League Organization."

The "Communist League Organization" was too good to be true. It was a functioning organization of a dozen Socialist members that feature Marx and Engels as members in good standing. Marx and Engels raced from Brussels to London to present their socialistic program to the group. It proved to be a timely offer, since Belgium authorities were knocking at their door and threatening incarceration. Marx and Engels were fortunate to find a safe haven in England. Engels rewrote the original manuscript of Communist rules; it was formatted just like a catechism. In London, Marx, with Engels's help, formatted it into a party platform for the Communist League. The group was so impressed that it immediately made them members and encouraged them to edit and submit their best theoretical and judicious political policies for future publication. This was going to be a harbinger for their secret Communist organization to attain political prominence. Before year's-end, Karl Marx and Friedrich Engels completed a preliminary manuscript of the book they called **"The Communist Manifesto."**

In 1850, Marx's living quarters were burglarized by a master German spy. The thief got away with a registry of names identifying the Communist League's active members. The registry was turned over to German and French government officials. The German police rounded up all the identified members of the Communist League, and held them for trial and sentencing in Germany.

The **Cologne Communist Trial** was conducted in Cologne, by the Prussian government. Eleven members of the Communist League were found guilty of criminal participation in the German Uprising of 1848. Seven of the eleven were sentenced to prison for six years.

After the trial ended, the Communist League was dissolved by the membership and faded into oblivion.

Together Karl Marx and Engels fled Germany, avoided prosecution and went back to London. It was there that the "The Communist Manifesto" was finally published. Although Marx was denied British citizenship, he stayed on to look for part-time work and concentrate on anti-capitalism by publishing a new book, "Das Kapital." It did not sell well. As for the original "Communist Manifesto," readers were few and book sales almost non-existent for many years

Broke, unemployed, and burdened with a family, his ambitions for social utopia proved elusive. Marx spent the last thirty-four years of his life living in the slums of London. He never did earn a living wage during in his lifetime. He subsisted on handouts, welfare, and cash support from Friedrich Engels until his death in 1883. Karl Marx's family lived with him in squalor and dire poverty. His wife and three children preceded him in death. In the bitter end. He was truly a man without a country, having been barred from every country he ever lived in. At his funeral service, he was officially confirmed a **"state-less person."** A man with no nationality. Friedrich Engels was there, to offer condolences and a eulogy for the benefit of the few mourners in attendance.

In North London, just beyond the gates of Highgate Cemetery, is the grave site of Karl Marx. Carved on the gray marble tombstone are these words: **"WORKERS OF All LANDS UNITE."**

CHAPTER 6

The Paris Commune

The year 1871 was one of great pain for Parisians. The recent defeat of the Second French Empire by Otto Von Bismarck of Germany left a bitter taste in the mouths of most Frenchmen, particularly the radical left. The city of Paris remained under siege after four months. Two million citizens suffered in poverty and near starvation. Even elitist author Victor Hugo of "Les Miserables" fame, succumbed to a diet of animals given to him by the Paris zoo.

March 18, 1871 marked the birth of the "Paris Commune." Revolt and command of the city meant removing the artillery guns of Montmartre. Without warning, National Guard troops guarding a two-hundred-gun battery high atop Montmartre turned their canons and used them to fire down against the Republican government in Paris. The heavy bombardment drove the opposition to retreat back to Versailles. With that violent action, the sovereign Commune of Paris was confirmed by thousands of exuberant rebels in defiance of their own government.

The word Commune might imply that this rebellion was solely an action by communist followers of Marx. Although there were some, the vast majority were middle-class individuals who simply wanted self-rule and to run their businesses in a purely capitalistic manner, without interference by a government that couldn't be trusted. Socialism was considered but never implemented. There were some rebellious cries of "Vive la Commune," by the Marxists. Karl Marx had written the "Communist Manifesto" twenty years earlier in Brussels just before being exiled, from both France and his homeland Germany.

The Commune worked fast to elect a Council Group, which included anarchists and some Communists, they conjured up the following principals by which Parisians would begin to operate;

Replace the ruling class with working class:

Advocate for a new secular state:

Suspension of all rent payments due to landlords:

Return items from pawnshops at no charge:

The right of employee ownership for enterprises abandoned by owners:

The Paris Commune was doomed to failure from the start. Those Versailles troops still loyal to the French Republic rejoined the head of state, Adolphe Thiers, and were battle ready for a second siege of Paris. History failed the Communards. Had not the fatal trials of the English colonies of Jamestown and Plymouth demonstrated how colonist lived and died under similar rules of government?

Within a week after formal organization, the Paris Commune fell under fierce attack. Adolphe Thiers had rebuilt and returned with an offensive force of 110,000 trained soldiers. The Communards had left a city bridge unguarded and promptly waved a white flag, but the battle raged on. Angry voices called out for the demolition of Notre Dame Cathedral. The cathedral survived, but the Commune forces succeeded to hang the Archbishop of Paris, a judge, two priests and two Jesuits were shot dead. There was a wholesale round up of religious orders.

Along the tree-lined boulevards of Paris, Frenchmen and women were fighting for their lives against other Frenchmen. Looting mobs methodically sacked hotels and robbed private residents, all while under the cover of a twenty-four-hour truce to evacuate wounded and starving Parisians. The disorganized Communards barricaded city streets, and in desperation burned public buildings and City Hall. They further expanded into a total scorched-earth defense; strong winds whipped the city of Paris into a blazing holocaust.

During the last week of May, the human bloodbath began in earnest. Adolphe Thiers's troops from Versailles stormed the city, crushing the Communards in street by street combat. The number of dead surpassed twenty thousand, fifteen thousand were arrested and seven thousand others were deported to Devil's Island for the rest of their lives.

On May 28, the last barricade of the Paris Commune fell to the government army's onslaught. In the aftermath a legion of Parisians faced the firing squad. Victors and vanquished had no forgiveness for each other--- all being angry French men and women.

The bygone Paris Commune, which was inaugurated on March 18, 1871 was utterly defeated six weeks later on May 28, 1871. For Paris, it was a disaster. A severe depression followed after all the bloodletting. The city continued to be under martial law (military) for five more years before peace returned to Paris, France.

In spite of the political failure and bloody debacle that desecrated Paris, Socialists from France and elsewhere soon adopted the Paris Commune legacy as their own epic event in order to advance their Socialist political agenda. The defeat of the Commune was otherwise universally declared a deathblow for the First International Communist Association, dominated by Karl Marx and Friedrich Engels. Nevertheless, following the devastating failure of the Paris Commune, Karl Marx publicly proclaimed, "Working-man's Paris with its new Commune will be forever celebrated as the glorious harbinger of a new society."

Otto Von Bismarck, first chancellor of Germany, strongly opposed Marxism and successfully had permanent anti-socialist laws passed in 1883. As fate would have it, Karl Marx quietly passed away the very same year.

CHAPTER 7

The First Soviet

The first great war of the twentieth century had just ended in 1905. Japanese military forces conquered the mighty Russian Army and annihilated the naval fleet of Nickolas II Romanov. The monarchy had foolishly assumed that the small island nation of Japan would not dare to oppose the superior military might of Imperial Russia. The unexpected defeat of Russia was swift and devastating. Japan's victory stunned the western world and absolutely shattered the confidence of all Russians. Nickolas II Romanov, emperor and autocrat of all that was Russian, lost the respect of his people. In the aftermath of the costly war, he was unable to satisfy the demands of hungry, unemployed workers suffering from an economic depression that swept the country. To make matters even worse, on an early Sunday morning in January, a procession of solemn looking protesters marched onto the grounds of the Royal Winter Palace in St. Petersburg. They intended to challenge the food shortages and serve a petition of grievances to Tsar Nicholas.

The Romanov's were out of the city and palace guards refused to let the massive crowd into the Palace Square. The protesters grew uncontrollable, so armed soldiers overreacted by firing into a raging mob. Some died and many were injured. The violence of this "**Bloody Sunday**" enraged the rank and file enough to take up arms against their own government. Ironically, the terrible incident was an idyllic crisis, or at least an opportunity not to be wasted by a radical group of Bolsheviks. This "Bloody Sunday" was a long awaited act of violence by opposing rebel leaders--- an act of civil intolerance to be utilized and rallied around. The rationale was that many additional members could be recruited for their narcissistic communistic cause. The current group of Bolsheviks were few in number, but they believed with additional actuated party members from Moscow, an overthrow of the besieged government would be possible in the capital city of St. Petersburg. Civil unrest and agitation continued all year.

It was early autumn in Moscow when a group of shop workers at Sytin's Print Works quarreled over a ridiculous salary problem with their shop boss. The argument was that they received no pay for type-setting punctuation marks. The workers normally did piece work and were paid for alphabet letters they set and printed but never received a single kopek for apostrophes. They demanded compensation for all piece-work, even punctuation marks. The angry workers further warned their manager to prepare himself to suffer the consequences of their newly organized "Soviet," (council) meeting on September 19, 1905. True to their word, the first ever Soviet council meeting took place at Sytin's Print Works.

The assemblage of workers was quick to launch a wide spread work stoppage. All the employees rose up and walked out in unison and adding to the drama, they were joined in sympathy by local bakery store employees. The next day thousands of belligerent workers took to the streets of Moscow.

News of the Sytin's print workers militant strike in Moscow spread like wildfire, all the way to the capital city of St. Petersburg. By September 24, the work stoppage spiraled into tens of thousands after fifty more major businesses closed down. Street riots broke out in Moscow. The escalation of the riots was rumored to be a planned action by a radical preacher-man named Leon Trotsky, the voice of the Bolsheviks. They said he pitched his propaganda every day. His pulpit was a hotel balcony high above the roadway; from there he would preach to mobs of strikers roving in the streets of St. Petersburg. His apparent mission was to inspire, enrage, and recruit as many fellow agitators as possible, particularly laborers from the Soviet Intercity Railroad. Audiences were large, and his followers were many.

By October 7, all the railroad workers of Russia proudly announced that their Soviet contingent was in the process of negotiating for a new improved proletarian government. Out of hiding, came yet another intrepid anarchist: Vladimir Lenin, a Marxist leader who also boldly took it upon himself to broadcast with a megaphone in the center of Red Square. His message was that new proletarian Soviets were about to be accepted as organs of the current revolutionary struggle against the monarchy. The term "soviet" became contemporary and connected to the existing power struggle by the working class. Within a week, a systematic shut-down of the railroads escalated into an unbelievable general strike that paralyzed transportation across the country. All commercial business and factory work came to a halt. Business offices and banks locked their doors. Power stations and the telegraph shut down. Strikers rioted in the urban areas of Moscow, St. Petersburg, Minsk, Odessa, and Kharkov. By this time two million people demonstrated in the streets: their battle cry was **"All power to the Soviets."** The Tsar's Cossacks (cavalrymen) totally lost control and charged the rioters with whips and sabers. Ultimately a gun battle broke out killing and wounding scores of people.

The Sytin's stoppage, born out of workers' complaint about not being paid to typeset punctuation marks, evolved from simple salary matter into a broad based militant rebellion. The truth was that Leon Trotsky's doctrinaire meetings had ignited activities into an explosive rebellion. By November, 1905, the bitter revolt persisted and the political backlash gained such incredible impetus that raging proletarians were threatening to put an end to three-hundred years of absolute rule by the Imperial Romanov dynasty.

Emperor Tsar Nicholas II Aleksandrovich Romanov, fearful of an imminent economic and military collapse, was hard-pressed to establish either a military dictatorship or a constitutional monarchy. Ultimately he chose to issue a conciliatory document, the **"October Manifesto,"** which was in fact a constitution promising to guarantee civil liberties--- freedom of speech, press, and assembly. At the height of the uprising, the tsar circulated his manifesto. Although it failed to sway the bellicose Marxist organizers, it did placate enough of the loyalists to reduce the body of revolutionary forces.

By December, loyal military forces crushed the revolutionary movement. Leon Trotsky and his comrades were arrested and found guilty of fostering civil disobedience and leading an armed rebellion; all were imprisoned in Siberia. Trotsky had previously been confined to Siberia for four years; he was known then by his birth name, Lev Bronshtein. In 1902, Leon Trotsky escaped from prison, abandoned his wife and children and changed his name. Lev Bronshtein, (a.k.a) Leon Trotsky, came to be known as the **"Eloquent Agitator"** of the First Soviet in 1905.

The Soviet revolt ended as abruptly as it had started. There remained scattered bands of Bolshevik protesters; they too were soon quelled by the government. Tsar Nicholas II kept his word and granted his people new freedoms, including freedom of speech, freedom of religion, and freedom of assembly. He also guaranteed that people would never be detained or charged without a fair trial before any imprisonment. On the other hand, Tsar Nicholas II never did reduce business working hours or grant any special wage increases--- not even a single kopeck for punctuation marks typeset by the printers at Sytin's Print Works.

The print workers' three-month strike had spiraled into an unprecedented sort of labor struggle. Initially, a trivial labor-management dispute at a small business germinated into a sensational political spectacle. However, the ensuing uprising was commandeered by two out of the ordinary Marxist activists; who were clever enough to create such political turmoil that their escapade intimidated the dominion of the Romanov monarchy. The turmoil ended when Tsar Nicholas II pacified the majority of Russians by creating a constitutional monarchy and granting parliament legislative powers. Many Russian citizens never wanted to overthrow the emperor. They simply wanted a more democratic type of government with improved living conditions. By year's end, Cossack troops arrested any malingering Bolshevik revolutionaries. Emperor Nicholas II signed his "October Manifesto" as a final act, hopefully to put an end to all memories of the Soviet Revolt of 1905.

As fate would have it; defeated Socialist claimed that the uprising was merely a dress rehearsal for future rebellions. Triumph was brief, they said; today's conquerors are often tomorrow's vanquished. Unlike Leon Trotsky, who was arrested, tried in court, and imprisoned in Siberia for encouraging an armed rebellion, his partner in crime, Vladimir Lenin, clean shaven, and incognito, managed to escape to Western Europe and find safe haven in Finland.

It was while conducting a conference for prospective Bolsheviks in Tammerfoers, Finland, that Lenin first met a comrade in arms, Joseph Stalin (Steel) alias Josef Dzhugashvili. At the time, he was a notorious bank robber who had escaped from a Siberian prison camp. It was Josef Dzhugashvili who sought the fellowship of the renown political fugitive Vladimir Lenin. Lenin viewed Dzhugashvili (Stalin) as a possible underground agent and being a successful bank robber, he could be a reliable money source for their cause.

Soon after, the two met again at yet another Bolshevik conference in Stockholm. This time Lenin fascinated Josef Dzhugashvili with stories of how he and Leon Trotsky successfully used reform-minded tactical methods to ignite civilian rage during the 1905 revolt, and how they honed action-plans goaded by class warfare, which were tried, rehearsed and reworked into effective prototypes to be executed again for future political uprisings. Trotsky was clever indeed. He outlined exactly what he called a sophisticated dialectical analysis of the laws that made it easy to motivate and control the simple-minded with emotive chants, rituals, and political propaganda. This was part and parcel at all the soviet meetings. Together they organized (labor unions) called Soviets and then explained about existing inbred hostility and antagonism between the classes of the haves against the pitiful have nots. Their charge was against all existing social and political order of things. **"The axis of all events, every thread ran towards it, every call to action emanated from it."** It was there in the fire of battle; that our singular mass organization was formed, the Soviets of workers deputies. But for now, revolutionary comrades must be patient and complete their training. Then and only then, when another revolution is indeed ripe, we will seize the pivotal moment. **"If we succeed in doing that, then the conflagrations will spread all over Europe."**

Lenin / Photo c. 1920
akg-images

"The Goal of Socialism is Communism"
Vladimir Lenin

CHAPTER 8

Bolshevik Rebellion 1917

The Russian Empire recovered and stabilized after the uprising in 1905. There occurred a renewed optimism for unity among the Russian people. Emperor Nicholas saw his monarchic duty as that of protecting autocracy and propagating Russia's Orthodox Christian faith. His reign and governance was once again distinguished by unprecedented industrial growth that outpaced all of Europe. In 1913, an elaborate state celebration was announced for the *Tercentenary of the House of Romanov.* This being the three-hundredth anniversary of the Romanov dynasty founded in 1613. A great reception took place in the majestic Winter Palace. After four festive days in St. Petersburg the celebration culminated along the roadway back to Moscow. It was a spectacular parade. Church bells rang out, and crowds of people lined the roadway, applauding the imperial family and saluting, Tsar Nicholas II. In view of all the public adoration, pomp, and circumstance, the Romanov dynasty appeared destined to reign supreme for another century.

The recent "October Manifesto" had effectively changed Russia into a constitutional monarchy, granting all Russians additional civil rights and a parliament with real legislative powers. Peter Stolypin was Tsar Nicholas's new unorthodox prime minister of the interior. His "farm land reform in 1906" created a new class of landowners by permitting masses of peasants to have personal ownership of acres of land, legally acquired from resident estate owners. Stolypin had great faith in the ability of struggling peasants. He took action before anyone knew it: Russia had an unheard of middle class of landowners. Stolypin moved three million peasants (serfs) out of their communal life and watched the new age farm owners prosper by the fruits of their labor.

Immigration virtually doubled with the completion of the emperor's contemporary Trans-Siberian Railway from Moscow to Vladivostok in 1916. Russian grain crops fed most of Europe. Russia was ranked as one of the world's great dynastic empires with an astonishing economy. Literacy was on the rise along with creative art, literature and musical virtuosity. This was a rarefied era of resplendent peace, productivity, and culture.

In five transitory years, the **"Stolypin Agrarian Land Reform"** proved to be the centerpiece of Russian reform. An evening of salutation and entertainment was arranged for the popular prime minister. Tsar Nicholas accompanied by Peter Stolypin his celebrated minister of reform, attended Rimsky Korsakov's opera *The Tale of Tsar Saltan*. During an intermission, Stolypin humbly reacted to the emperor's many compliments, saying, "I must tell you, my idea for private ownership of land was shared by others. My friend, the famed author and philosopher, **Fyodor Dostoevsky,** once told me, **"If you want to transform humanity for the better, or to turn beasts into humans, give them land and you will reach your goal."** At evening's end, Peter graciously thanked the emperor for such a grand evening. He reassured Nicholas II, **"Give the state twenty years of peace, internal and external, and you will not recognize present-day Russia."** Peter's grandiose prediction was not to be and was incredibly ill-timed.

On this historic night, a demon of death lurked in the shadows of the Kiev Opera House. Tsar Nicholas, accompanied by his two daughters, exited the theatre along with Peter Stolypin. Suddenly, out of the shadows, leaped a wild-eyed devil firing two bullets into the prime minister. Stolypin fell hard, face-down on the lobby floor of the opera house. Tsar Nicholas leaned over the motionless body sprawled in a pool of blood, mindful that this could be the end of Russia's greatest statesman. Only Stolypin had the genius to detail reform programs and the ability to produce spectacular results. The emperor realized with agonizing clarity that he had a major catastrophe on his hands; Peter was dying and his secure autocracy was suddenly in jeopardy. Still barely clinging to life several hours later at a nearby hospital. Stolypin's dying words were, **"I am happy to die for my Tsar." He made the sign of the cross… and died.**

The assassin was Dmitri Bogrov, a member of the Socialist Revolutionary Party. He was captured and hanged ten days later. Lenin activists began agitating for an armed revolution. Peter Stolypin's reform program, which had emancipated ordinary peasants, and awarded them private land ownership, was vehemently opposed by Lenin's Socialists. They cursed the thought of a middle-class society. **Poor peasants had been suddenly turned into prosperous farmers, called Kulaks. There was no place for any of this, not in a totalitarian country.**

As feared, within days the national reform programs began to collapse. Tsar Nicholas tried, but lost control of most of the important matters without the help of his former prime minister. He placed unqualified men into key government positions after taking rash advice from his wife. Tsarina Alexandra, who was ill-advised by Rasputin a self proclaimed holy man.

Grigori Rasputin, reputed to be a Russian mystic and faith healer was inexplicably the personal adviser to Tsarina Alexandra. Rasputin's very presence incited public scorn against the Romanov's. Russia was already abounding with malcontents, who alleged that the monarchy was reneging on many of its promised civil liberties. Half of the country's workers were on strike. Making matters worse, the First World War (The Great War) exploded across the continent. Tsar Nicholas II decided to take direct command of the Russian Army while Tsarina Alexandra assumed responsibility for domestic matters. A military leader he was not, a devoted family man indeed, and to those who knew him best, Tsar Nicholas II was considered the most civilized man in Europe. But, the war under his charge quickly lapsed into a calamity, similar to the recent failed Russo-Japanese War. Tsar Nicholas, as supreme commander of the Russian Army was blamed for excessive troop casualties and hyper inflationary war costs that effectively kept the people's food bins empty. A small loaf of bread was not affordable for many half-starved peasants. Living conditions and loyalties were deteriorating rapidly. Their constitutional monarchy certainly worked well for a good while. However, after a decade of economic growth, improved civil liberties and all former enemies of the state either exiled or in prison. Russia's era of peace and productivity slid backward into a state of lawlessness and war. **The stage was set for a royal tragedy, with a raft of bad actors waiting in the wings.**

Empirical Russia was on the verge of collapse. The vindictive Bolsheviks' long wait was over; now was their time to seize the moment. The exiled Marxist, Vladimir Lenin had already campaigned remotely from Switzerland advising soldiers to rise up and turn their "Russian imperialistic war into a civil war." He circulated propaganda pamphlets urging troops to turn their rifles against their own officers and start a Socialist revolution. Wasting no time, the Bolshevik echelon headed straight for Russia. First to arrive was Lenin, oddly enough with considerable help from enemy German soldiers. They knew very well that his rebellious tactics would work to their advantage as Germany was losing a bloody downhill trench war against England and France, in addition to the Russians. This was a strategic move by the Germans to covertly ship the mutinous Vladimir Lenin across the Swiss border inside a sealed railroad boxcar bound for Moscow.

Alive and back in Moscow, Lenin was contacted by escaped fugitive Leon Trotsky (a.k.a. Bronshtein) and later by the Bank robber, Joseph Stalin (a.k.a. Dzhugashvili). Trotsky who spoke only Russian and German, unexpectedly was located overseas in America perform- ing as a keynote speaker in the company of fifty comrades from the "1905" insurgency. All were members of the Committee of Russian Revolutionists exiled in the United States. A group of sympathetic collaborators, or "useful idiots as he called them," entertained him, provided accommodations and secretly slipped in two million dollars' of gold for his special needs back in Russia. The generous financial aid came from New York banker's who had provided financial aid during the first Russian Soviet rebellion.

After savoring a month of decadent American high life, Trotsky steamed from the port of New York City hell-bent on getting to Russia, but much to his displeasure he was apprehended on the high seas by British naval police. They boarded his ship and rerouted the entire group to Halifax, Nova Scotia, where Trotsky was held and charged as a wanted crimi- nal foreign revolutionist. After four weeks of intense questioning Leon Trotsky was released by higher authorities. He departed aboard the S.S.Christiania flaunting a prestigious American passport personally authorized and signed by none other than the president of the United States, Woodrow Wilson. Trotsky and his entire entourage landed back in Russia emboldened with $20 (gold) seed money entrusted to him by a banker who was originally of the House of Rothschild in Frankfort, Germany but had long since immigrated to America and ultimately became a prominent New York banker.

On arrival in Russia, Trotsky was eager to collaborate with Lenin. Being the gifted orator that he was, he routinely mesmerized gangs of workers and peasants with his dynamic speeches. He cited all the evils of class warfare, spiked with propaganda slogans pledging, "Peace, land and bread," and then wrapped it all up with the riotous group shouting, "**All power to the Soviets, All power to the Soviets!** "

By February 1917, a widespread labor strike shut down the capital city of Petrograd. Once more, violent brawls broke out between strikers and local police who by this time opened fire at raging rioters. The action was so fierce that the army was called in to help, but instead the soldiers became sympathetic and took the side of the rioters. The Russian Parliament hurriedly setup a hapless temporary government, but it was too late to be effective.

Riotous strikes and political anarchy raged everywhere, overpowering the military. The ranking military officers only recourse was to implore Emperor Nicholas to abdicate. On March 1, 1917, after being advised by military leaders, and unyielding Bolsheviks. Tsar Nicholas II Romanov with deep sorrow consented to abdicate the royal throne after three hundred years of Romanov's reigning Russia. His last desperate plea was **"May the Lord God help Russia."**

The aftershock gave Nicholas pause; he recalled how as a young boy his grandfather Alexander II, often recited to him a speech by President Abraham Lincoln: "Familiarize yourself with the chains of bondage and you prepare your own limbs to wear them. Accustomed to trample on the rights of others, you have lost the genius of your own independence and become the fit subjects of the first cunning tyrant who rises among you."

His admonition was offered at the time of the American Civil War. At the time, President Lincoln and Emperor Alexander II politically shared economic and currency problems with the Rothschild bankers. Lincoln like President Andrew Jackson before him refused to grant financial control of United States banking and currencies to a federal central bank. Both were also challenged with fierce civil strife.

Emperor Alexander II was sympathetic and, lacking any European allies, offered President Lincoln military assistance for his Union forces during the civil war. The tsar went so far as to issue a public warning that if England or France actively interfered in the American Civil War, Russia would consider it an act of war and take the side of President Lincoln. Two Russian fleets impudently steamed into two American harbors during the war in 1863, one docked in San Francisco Bay and the other in New York harbor. Their Baltic Fleet was greeted with enthusiasm but never used for naval combat. The only benefit to Lincoln's Union forces was that of a well-timed morale booster and an epic show of Russian friendship to America.

As for negating the "chains of bondage," Emperor Alexander II and President Lincoln were fellow emancipators. Russian serfs were freed in 1859 and President Lincoln ended American slavery in 1865. Alas thereafter, both men being larger than life figures were cruelly assassinated. Foreign relations with Russia remained relatively neutral during the years leading up to the Bolshevik Rebellion of 1917. The Romanov dynasty of three hundred years ceased to exist in March 1917. Emperor Nicholas II Aleksandrovich Romanov along with Empress Alexandra, and their five children remained under house arrest at their Imperial Winter Palace in Russia.

The Red Army was now under the command of **Commissar of War Leon Trotsky.** He prepared his troops for an all-out offensive to expand their own borders while the "Great War" (World War 1) raged on and madness was encompassing all of Europe. Communist's persecution of Christians, the burning of Russian Orthodox churches, and the killing of priests and clergy became procedural acts of inhumanity. Forced labor camps were another act of dehumanization, devised for utilization of compliant humans as tools of labor solely for the greater good of the state. The apparent ambition of the secular Communist regime was no more or less than to deny God and overthrow both religion and all existing social mores.

In May of 1917, newspapers reported a phenomenal religious apparition was witnessed in Fatima, Portugal. Three shepherd children of C ova Da Iria near Fatima were visited by an apparition of Mary, Blessed Mother of Jesus Christ, calling for an urgent need for consecration of Russia. **The children told of several secret prophesies about a future Second World War and a prediction that Russia would do great harm to humanity by abandoning the Christian faith and embracing communistic totalitarianism.** The Blessed Mother had promised the three children that; they would be able to prove her appearance to others with yet another visible miracle on October 13, 1917. The possession of such profound secrets proved to be a scathing trial for the three young children. The word spread like wild-fire and crowds continued to grow. On the promised date of October 13, 1917, once again the apparition appeared for the children as promised only this time seventy thousand spectators stood in the open fields in torrential rain to witness the event. The Lisbon daily newspapers O'Suculo and O Dia reported the following story. *"Before the astonished eyes of the crowd of 70,000 people, whose aspect was biblical as they stood bare-headed, eagerly searching the sky, the sun trembled, made sudden incredible movements outside of all cosmic law--- the sun danced according to the expression of the people. The people wept and prayed with uncovered heads and suddenly dried clothes, all in the presence of a miracle they had awaited."*

The fact was three small children had been assured of validation by the Blessed Virgin months in advance of the miraculous event, and **"The Miracle of the Sun"** inexplicably occurred just as predicted and was witnessed, and described as miraculous by seventy thousand people at the event. The religious apparition was judged truly prophetic by most Europeans nearing a breaking point of warfare.

Miracle or not, two weeks after the Miracle of Fatima in 1917, a fierce revolution was set in motion in Moscow, Russia. An attack force of Bolsheviks stormed Red Square, and overpowered the entire city before announcing that the St. Petersburg Soviet was Russia's new parliamentary government. Within a month, Bolsheviks (*Communists*) seized full power. Leon Trotsky made a military decision to officially withdraw his subordinated Red Army out of World War I, only to do an about-face, and command the army to attack and kill fellow countrymen in a contemptuous civil war pitting his Bolshevik Red Army against the (anti-Bolshevik/Loyalist) White Army.

The entire royal Romanov family was abruptly uprooted by the Bolsheviks, and moved far away from their familiar surroundings at the Winter Palace, first to the governor's mansion in Tobolsk, Siberia, and then, for some strange reason, once again in the summer to an unfamiliar Ipatiev house in Yekaterinburg. The cloak and dagger movements were allegedly to protect the royal family from the desperate White Russian Army. The untold truth is that the majority of Russians still honored and remained loyal to Nicholas II. The White Russian Army was essentially fighting to restore Nicholas II to the throne. The royal family began to wonder why their actual location was always kept secret from all public inquiries. Their suspicions were soon validated.

It was past midnight on July 17, 1918, and the entire royal family was awakened; His Majesty Nicholas II, the aging empress, four charming daughters, their young hemophiliac son, and their domestics were calmly herded downstairs into a musty basement room of their detention house. Without explanation or the benefit of any tribunal, judge, or jury, the entire Romanov family, senselessly murdered, one by one in a putrid storm cellar... by order of Vladimir Lenin. Twelve cold-blooded assassins then routinely murdered the elderly valet, two servants, the family doctor, and even the children's dog. All eleven victims were shot at close range and, for assurance, painstakingly bayoneted. The mutilated bodies were bagged and buried beneath the roadway path leading to a nearby forest.

Nicholas II and Family / Photo, c.1915
akg-images

Yesteryear's victors of the "First Soviet Revolt" were at last vanquished by a minority of contemptuous Bolsheviks. Ironically, the Romanov monarchy over the years had always granted their deadliest foes the benefit of a fair and legal trial. Yet, Vladimir Lenin, without hesitation, vindictively ordered their mass execution without any hearing or trial, and not just the ruler, but all remaining family members, young, old and any associates he could catch. By 1919, of the remaining relatives, seventeen more Romanov's were hunted down and murdered by Lenin's Communist henchmen.

The gruesome slaughter of the Romanov family in 1918 eclipsed the distant memory of an earlier conspiracy to assassinate a Romanov Tsar. It was thirty years earlier when Lenin's older brother Alex Ulyanov, himself a notorious anarchist, was captured and put on trial as the prime conspirator and bomb maker used in a political conspiracy to assassinate Emperor Alexander II. When found guilty during a raucous trial, he defiantly refused to plead for clemency. He alone was executed by hanging while his conspirator sister along with a younger brother, Vladimir were spared. **Vladimir the image of his older brother remained an estranged youth with a nihilistic hatred for the existing social structure.**

Could it be that the massacre of the entire Romanov family was one man's compulsion for vengeance or an improbable coincidence that after thirty years Tsar Alexander's grandson Nicholas II and his entire family were murdered in cold blood by orders of none other than the Bolshevik, Vladimir Lenin? It was he who in fact changed his name and identity from Vladimir Ulyanov to Vladimir Lenin years ago to avoid future arrest or possible recognition following his notorious brother's execution. How better to avenge a reigning monarch than to incite a mob of crazed insurgents with Marxist socialism, further empowered by the rabble rousing semantics of Leon Trotsky and Vladimir Lenin's utopian versions of a glorified Communist state.

The regime of bloodletting and terror raged on. It was an obsessed fringe group of Bolsheviks that emerged in full charge of the government, not the monarchy of old. Vladimir Lenin, leader of the Bolsheviks, unleashed his own Marxist-Lenin dictatorship in Russia. Instead of "Peace, Land and Bread" as he promised. It was deceit, perverse cruelty and a devastating civil war that sucked the life out of an already starving society. The docile party members had believed the utopia propaganda spewed by the pseudo-intellectuals Lenin and Trotsky. But the Bolsheviks' true objective was Nihilism. Their plan was a deviant doctrine, a negation of all moral principles. Destruction of all existing political, social, and religious order was their convoluted solution to a more perfect political and social government. On August 11, 1918 Lenin issued a **"Hanging Order,"** his specific orders were, **"set an example by hanging a hundred of the bloodsuckers so the public sees, publish their names... the entire revolution demands this... Yours, Lenin."**

They viewed politics of the past as proletarian roadblocks to freedom. In its place their system of social and economic communism would reward all adherents a future of political enlightenment and a lifetime of social order as determined by a new totalitarian government.

Leon Trotsky became War Commissar of the Red Army and president of the Supreme War Council even though, he never served or had any sort of past military experience. Nevertheless, he instituted compulsory conscription and never hesitated to conduct field tribunals and summary execution of any military officers who failed to display ample zeal. Commissar Trotsky also found it expedient to order obstinate political figures executed. Ultimately he commandeered a gigantic army of five million troops. The local civil war proved to be a brutal struggle; atrocities were unbridled by Trotsky's forces. For two and a half years the Bolshevik (Red Army) fought desperately to survive against powerful but fewer Russian Cossacks. The Red Army confiscated grain for their troops while millions of women, children, and aged were left to starve during the Volga famine of 1921. The entire country was in ruins before the killing stopped and beyond all belief, Leon Trotsky's Red Army somehow defeated the White (anti-Bolshevik) Army. The Bolshevik name was officially changed to the Communist Party. Russia was formally renamed the Union of Soviet Socialist Republics (USSR). The Red Army (Bolshevik) won the civil war and with it total control of the new Socialist republic.

The red, white and blue flag of old Russia was torn down. A new red flag marked with a hammer and sickle now flew over the capital. Unfortunately, there were no residual spoils of war to salvage: living conditions were catastrophic at best following the war. The civil war casualties alone reckoned nine million dead Russians and another two-fold of half dead and wounded. Even worse, the everlasting food famine claimed six million men, women, and children who starved to death. Lenin and Trotsky exhibited a perverse contempt for the sufferings of their fellow countrymen and mercilessly terminated agitators. Trotsky declared: *"In a country where the sole employer is the State, opposition means death by slow starvation. The old principle: Who does not work shall not eat, has been replaced by a new one: Who does not obey shall not eat."*

Portrait of Leon Trotsky / Photo, c.1920
akg-images / Pictures From History

CHAPTER 9

The Hammer and the Sickle

A triumphant Communist flag was conceived during the Russian Revolution of 1917. The mandated revolutionary flag featured the images of a hammer, sickle, and star embossed on a blood-red fabric, all symbolic of the new totalitarian government. Gone were the outdated symbols of a tercentenary, replaced by blatant symbols of a new age Communist revolution. The hammer was symbolic of an urban laboring class, the sickle, a tool of peasant farmers, and the gold star for the inevitable achievement of global Soviet socialism. The celebrated flag-waver of the hammer and sickle banner was none other than merciless Red Army War Commissar, Leon Trotsky, who had one million battle-seasoned troops standing by to do whatever was bloody well necessary for the progression of Soviet Socialist communism.

The neophyte government set up a system of oppressive rules steeped in fear and terror. Vladimir Lenin's Communist ideology banned all religious theology. Lenin, being an Antichrist, rationalized that **"religion was the opiate of the masses."** As secular leader of the masses, he ordered an immediate halt to the worship of God or any type of religious activities. Also there was an immediate nationalization of all existing business. Central government officials would assume control of all industrial production and subsistence. Private property ownership of farmland ended, and with it would be the confiscation of most private land and work tools. Collectivization of agriculture was the new way of the future.

Lenin appointed only avowed Communist atheists for his personal quasi-cabinet members. Russia, being a God-fearing country with a long history of Christianity (AD *988*) was then sadistically turned into the first totally atheist state in the modern world. The religious faithful were anguished when fifty thousand of their Christian Orthodox churches were pillaged, closed, and burned to the ground, and then they were forced to stand by in shock while priests and ministers were murdered.

The altars of Christianity were desecrated and servants of Christ massacred. Millions of God fearing Christians were slain by this revolutionary totalitarian government.

Trotsky, a compelling public speaker in his own right, devoted much of his time spewing Communist propaganda across the turbulent continent. If allowed, he would rant every day to smitten crowds of laborers, soldiers, oppressed families and rowdy street urchins. The interaction between the explosive orator and his audience was charged as though it was a circus event. He would chide them on: "Let your soviets of workers, soldiers, and peasants, declare the righteous way for peace, bread, and liberty! Trotsky said,"Your in a war. A war of poor oppressed classes dogged by those domineering upper classes... Mind you, the Russian Soviet revolution is the prologue of a world revolution." Trotsky's defiant propaganda tour included Germany and Italy in spite of both being hostile anticommunist communities

Adolph Hitler at the time had democratic Germany on the brink of anarchy as a result of his bigoted master-race book, "Mein Kampf," in which he identified the Communist Party as a primary enemy of Germany. In Italy, Benito Mussolini's Fascist Party exhorted Italian nationalism. He too publicly denounced Marxist socialism and its ridiculous class-warfare arguments as an out-of-date failure. The animosity between conflicting ideologies turned violent. Gangs of Italian Fascists routinely attacked Soviet Communists in wild street fights and often strong-armed secret Communist meetings with clubs and weapons. Also the repulsion of active Communist organizations was equally fierce in Germany.

While Trotsky visited European enclaves spreading his brand of Communist propaganda, Joseph Stalin failed to tell Trotsky that their mutual leader, Lenin had been critically ill for many months while under his care. Lenin died of a massive hemorrhage in January 1924. The untold story was that during the last year of Vladimir Lenin's life, he had a series of three strokes, and being debilitated, he remained a sequestered patient under the exclusive care of Stalin, who arbitrarily took over all of Lenin's executive duties. This was a devious ruse by Stalin to boost his credibility over all of his own party competitors and to prove that he alone was Lenin's favorite and most loyal friend. However, Stalin was unaware that Lenin, while racked with pain and fearing sudden death, worried greatly about the future progress of his unproven Communist experiment. Secretly, Lenin wrote a sincere letter revealing his anxieties for the Communist Party, but worse than that, how he personally had witnessed Stalin's character flaws and, in particular, his dangerous incompetence. He found a way to mail his profound feelings directly to the Central Communist Committee revealing Joseph Stalin as an impetuous, ruthless man and not any-where the leader that Trotsky was. Shortly thereafter on his deathbed Lenin admitted, "**I committed a great error. My nightmare is to have the feeling that I'm lost in an ocean of blood from the innumerable victims. It is too late to return... save our country.**"

Trotsky no longer a confidant of Stalin was woefully unaware of how much conditions had changed and did not attend Lenin's funeral. In his typical arrogance, Trotsky like most party members continued to under-estimate Joseph Stalin's ruthless cunning. Before they knew it, this megalomaniac in his insatiable lust for power unbelievably proceeded to eliminate, one by one, all potential rivals for the Communist party leadership. As for Trotsky, Stalin successfully removed his perennial adversary from power in 1923. Trotsky barely survived multiple assassination attempts before escaping from Europe in fear for his life. For years he was doggedly hunted far and wide across Europe, Asia and North America by Russian agents. It was a quiet little village near Mexico City where, Ramon, a Communist Spaniard, found and befriended Trotsky. Unfortunately, his new Spanish friend Ramon turned out to be a messenger of death for Stalin. Ramon Mercader worked for the Soviet underground as a Communist assassin. Mexican police found Leon Trotsky with a bloody ice axe impaled in his skull: nearby was a copy of his book "**The Revolution Betrayed."** Ramon, the assassin never got past the Mexico City prison, where he stayed for twenty years before returning to Moscow. He survived and was eventually awarded his country's highest medal, a **Hero of the Soviet Union** and permanent placement of honor in a Moscow museum.

Similar to the injustice of the Royal Romanov family murders. The infamous Commissar Leon Trotsky in the bitter end also had no trial judge to hear his plea for life. But then again, he and Stalin always did mutually agree that, ---- **"the ends justified the means."**

Owing to the errant ideology of itinerant philosopher Karl Marx; Communistic socialism was hypothetically their scientific means to achieve a utopian life style for all of human society. Instead, under Lenin and Trotsky and Stalin, life was cheap and death rampant. The ends always justified the means for the good of the state. This new socialistic credo denied the most basic rights of humanity: life, liberty, and ownership of private property. Karl Marx's communistic manifesto was at best a sterile economic theory barring the practical expediency of Lenin and the oratory of Trotsky. Lenin realized his Bolshevik revolution would merely remain a transient political faction without some dynamic paradigm to ensure that his brand of communism had sustainability.

Note: Five hundred years earlier, Nicole Machiavelli an Italian, first wrote. "That the ends – no matter how immoral—justify the means for preserving political authority." His political theorist writing of "The Prince" further advised that a prince can fight by the law (the way of men) or by force (the way of beasts). And it will benefit the prince to act like a beast--- to act like the cunning and deceitful fox or the cruelly powerful lion.

In the 1870's, two young men, Vladimir Lenin and his older brother Alex swore allegiance to a creed of twenty-six heinous rules for revolutionists. Faithfully, when Lenin became the mentor of the Communist Party, he made sure both Trotsky and Stalin understood the same twenty-six general rules found in the **"Catechism of a Revolutionary."** These were dogmatic rules used to maintain political control and to ensure sustainability for the Communist movement during the twentieth century.

The book was published by Lenin, but the real author was Sergei Nechayev in 1869. Nechayev was a militant leader of an early anarchist movement in Moscow. His message, "Our task is terrible, total, universal, and merciless destruction, with any crime or treachery necessary to effect the downfall of the prevailing order." Nechayev was captured, tried, and sentenced in 1873 for the brutal murder of a fellow member of his terrorist group. He had purposely beat and killed Ivanovich Ivanov in the presence of comrades; and there was method to his madness. He gained their allegiance but also incriminated them as spellbound witnesses who assisted in his criminal act of murder. Then he rationalized it all with the familiar maxim---**"The ends justify the means"**.

Nechayev managed to escape from Moscow authorities before moving on to London. It was there that he published another journal called "The Commune." He recklessly continued to incite subversive movements until arrested in Zurich, Switzerland. He was extradited back to St. Petersburg, Russia, where he was found guilty of murder and sentenced to twenty years of hard labor. Even as a prisoner Nechayev found ways to assist in political eruptions with another anarchist group called the *People's Will*, led by Lenin's older brother, Alex who was the master-mind behind the plan to assassinate Tsar Alexander II.

Sergei Nechayev, after many years of solitary confinement, died of consumption and scurvy in 1882. His book the "Catechism of a Revolutionary" had turned into an evil dogma that sadistically warped the psyche of radicals throughout Russia. Lenin made sure Nechayev's soul-shattering covenant with death and destruction was published and read by all Communist Party leaders.

The city of Petrograd was renamed Leningrad three days after Lenin's death. In the meantime Joseph Stalin continued to methodically dispose of political rivals and further consolidated his power base until he alone emerged as the unopposed dictator of the Soviet Union. Stalin was a poorly educated Georgian. Not being well versed in Marx and Engels's theories of revolution or various Communist dictates, Stalin strictly followed Lenin's doctrines and political views. He immediately had history books rewritten to show how he had led the revolution with Lenin and Trotsky, although he was imprisoned most of the time. Lenin initiated Russian Communism, but Joseph Stalin's compulsion was to be history's most feared Communist dictator.

Lenin's dictatorship began by murdering the Romanov family and was perpetuated by unrequited terror and mass murders. Stalin intended to build upon the base that Lenin established. As a first act he arranged for the murders of all the Bolsheviks who had seized power in 1917. His reasoning was **"Scientifically speaking, the dictatorship of the proletariat is a power which is restricted by no laws, hampered by no rules, and based directly on violence."**

These megalomaniac's psychotic acts marked the inauguration of a regime of brutality that served as a forewarning of future mass executions for nonconformists. Stalin launched a Five Year Plan and domestic policy that exacted unrealistic industrialization quotas and collectivization of all farm-land hoping to transform the Soviet Union into an enduring socialistic state. All industries and services were nationalized while all privately owned farms and land were confiscated into giant government collective farms, freeing up idled peasants for work in state industrial labor camps. Wealthier farmers (kulaks) and peasants who resisted government changes suffered a catastrophic famine and genocide. Stalin's collectivization program commenced with the grotesque mass murders of tens of thousands of men, women and children.

All private ownership of property came to an end after another five million Russian kulaks (resisting farmers) were transported to Siberian labor camps never be heard from again. Stalin's forced collectivization of agriculture, forced slave labor camps, and new factories ultimately converted the Soviet Union (USSR) into an industrial economy at the morbid cost of millions of human lives. Stalin's minority party of elitists ruled and subjugated the majority, which included all non-elitist classes of society.

The neighboring Ukrainians clung desperately to their independence from Soviet Union domination. Stalin had other plans for them. He wanted the fertile Ukraine farmlands for part of his Socialist agriculture collectivism, and their existing grain supplies would feed his own starving people. He ordered all Ukraine borders to be securely sealed by his Red Army and monitored by the Soviet Secret Police. He then set into motion a scheme to create a famine in the Ukraine using methods that had worked with the kulaks in Russia. Secret Soviet Police raided Ukrainian farm-houses, seizing stored food and leaving families without a morsel. Starvation was immediate throughout the Ukraine, while without fail the police and Communist Party officials continued to be well fed. Before long, state Socialist programs were in full force and the nation's village farmers (kulaks) were gone. Stalin achieved his Five Year Plan objectives, but 25 percent of the total population including three million children perished for the sake of his absurd political experiment of "collectivization and Industrialization."_

Ludwig von Mises of Austria was an acclaimed economist and social philosopher of twentieth century. Early on, as chief economic adviser to the Austrian government, he warned the world that the heralded socialistic "New Era" prosperity was a sham and would end in a banking panic and economic depression. He also defiantly published his article, "Economic Calculation in the Socialist Commonwealth." The essay methodically proved that it would be impossible for any Socialist planning board to plan a modern economic system since a pricing and costing system requires an exchange of property titles and therefore private property in the means of production. Without private ownership of land, as in collectivism and capital goods, socialism would be disastrous and eventually fail.

Mises emphatically proclaimed, **"The expansion of free markets, the division of labor, and private capital investment is the true path to prosperity.** The captain is the consumer; they determine precisely what should be produced in what quality, and what quantities. Capitalists can only preserve and increase their wealth best by filling the orders of the consumers because the consumers are their bosses.

And if history could prove and teach us anything, it would be that private ownership of the means of production is a necessary requisite of civilization and material well-being. Only nations committed to the principle of private property have risen above penury and produced science, art, and literature."

Unfortunately, alone during the rise of dogmatic dictators, Mises' scientific refutation of socialistic economics was a valiant effort but was stifled by Socialist adversaries who labeled him a fool extremist. Ludwig von Mises' Socialism: "An Economic and Sociological Analysis" was an intellectual read that also was discredited by political foes as being another decadent, laissez-faire, capitalistic concept.

Unchallenged and feared, Joseph Stalin reigned supreme, as the new general secretary of the Communist Party and aimed to be history's most notorious protractor of the Communist (Socialist) cause. Some regarded him as a cunning politician, at least in the sense that he was a master of deception with a unique ability to fool others into underestimating him. He permeated a cult of idolatry by means of party-line propaganda programs, bold poster art, and larger-than-life statues of himself prominently displayed in public squares throughout Russia. Censored artists and poets were instructed to glorify him for bringing about abundant grain crops and modern factories. **Moreover, the unmentionable but ever-present sphere of Stalin's motivating was that of sheer terror and killing.**

Driven by paranoia, Stalin built a worldwide spy network infiltrating many top level foreign governments right on down to local neighbors spying on each other. And when the NKVD, Stalin's Secret Service Police visited suspect neighbors, they mysteriously vanished.

He targeted brutal terror purges of his own people. No one was exempt, not even the military. Stalin ordered the summary execution of thousands of his own military troops including shooting eighty-one of his top-ranking Russian generals and admirals. The slaughter continued, with thousands of suspected non-loyal fellow Communists and party officials executed. The "**purge**" never stops; killings of the masses soared into the millions, and he herded millions more off to forced labor camps (Gulags) in Siberia--- never to return.

Portrait of Stalin / Photo, 1943
akg-images / Interfoto / awkz

Stalin worked hard to create a standing army the size that the world had never seen before. Millions of troops were drafted but his total military force was ill-equipped and untrained to the point of serving early-on as gun fodder for the powerful German war machine. Russian foot soldiers were mostly unarmed and untrained due to the scarcity of experienced field officers or generals. Unfortunately, Stalin in a fit of paranoia had all officers who served under Trotsky executed. His massive army was not yet as successful as Lenin or Trotsky's had been.

In 1941 Adolph Hitler of Germany betrayed his short-term ally Joseph Stalin. He dispatched the full force of the German war machine: armored tank divisions and ground troops charged eastward across the Russian borders. The German Wehrmacht easily overwhelmed the dazed enemy and in short order occupied much of Russia. The Second World War was underway. Russia barely escaped annihilation only by virtue of gaining new allies, along with America's monumental Lend-Lease program that supplied and delivered heavy armaments, military weapons, munitions, material goods, and food supplies. Early in the war, a decisive battle for control of the Atlantic Ocean was successfully turned around by American forces with British support. The Nazis (German National Socialists) failed to conquer Moscow, Leningrad, and Stalingrad due to a severe Russian winter and strategic blockades of their gasoline, munitions, and air force.

When it came to fierce combat against the Italians or the Japanese forces, Russia never helped even though it was an ally of the United States and Britain. After the U.S. Air Force bombed the obliterated German defenses, Russian troops were able to march into Berlin and Vienna. Communists far and wide decreed that it was Communist Russia that liberated Europe and defeated Germany while the Americans went on to fight against Japan. In 1945, an American bomber dropped the world's first Atomic bomb on Hiroshima Japan. The frightful force of the Bomb stunned the entire world: however Japanese leaders refused to surrender when given prior warnings. Three days later, a second bomb was dropped on the city of Nagasaki. By then, Emperor Hirohito of Japan agreed to an unconditional surrender.

Premier Stalin was eager to expand his brand of communism in Asia and seized the moment. Suddenly on August 10, 1945, as the last embers of war smoldered out, Joseph **Stalin declared war against the people of Japan and rushed Russian troops into Manchuria and, Korea and aligned himself with Mao Tse-tung. He and joined**

in Mao's goal to conquer and change Mainland China into another communist counterpoise to United States.

All combat fighting in the Far East ended four days later on August 14, 1945. But **three days later, the Korean Peninsula was divided along the 38th parallel as another ominous divide-and- conquer maneuver. Soviet troops immediately took control of North Korea, and declared it a Communist government territory never to be confused with the American military occupation of South Korea and its non-Communist government,** ruled by Syngman Rhee, a native islander. By September, the convulsing guns of war fell silent, soon after the second mushroom cloud gave way to azure skies. The world's most destructive war had finally flamed out in the land of the rising sun.

Glorious cries of joy abated the years of carnage and unbearable misery. Dreams of peace and prosperity filled the minds of most. Still there were mixed emotions for the legions of wounded souls and, of course, there was no shared victory or joy for the millions of sacrificed lives.

The end of the Second World War was a requiem event for the world, but not according to the Communist Dictator Joseph Stalin. The spoils of war were there for his taking. Defeat of the German war-machine opened many of the gates in Europe, much to the benefit of Stalin's plan for a Union of Soviet Socialist Republics. He was quick to claim strategic rights to East Germany, Romania, Albania, Hungary, Yugoslavia, Poland, Bulgaria, Czechoslovakia, part of Finland, even territories of Korea, Japan and China.

So much for peace. **The flag of totalitarian communism--- the hammer, sickle and star was going to be flown in many countries.** The Soviet Union's influence was a growing danger to the world. Winston Churchill used a defining phrase to describe the changing political situation: "An iron curtain has descended across the Continent"...

"The Communist parties, which were very small in all the Eastern States of Europe, have been raised to preeminence and power far beyond their numbers and are seeking everywhere to obtain totalitarian control." There after ideological and economic rivalries intensified. The prolonged state of hostility marked the beginning of a long-lasting political and military conflict commonly known as, **"The Cold War."**

CHAPTER 10

Political Pseudoscience

Socialism is a pseudo-science that propagates an ideology of anarchy, not political science. There is little or no evidence of a successful Socialist Economic System of Government. The Totalitarian social/ economic governance system employed by Vladimir Lenin failed upon onset. Lacking in logical references or reliable economic solutions in general, failure was inevitable. It resulted in poverty, misery, tyranny, genocide and the bloodiest century in history.

Many years ago, sage Pierre S. DuPont said it best: "**Bad logicians have committed more involuntary crimes than bad men have done intentionally."** Karl Marx pitifully lacked any fiscal knowledge or any real work experience he could relate to. Furthermore, neither Vladimir Lenin nor Joseph Stalin (an ex-bank robber) grasped macro-economic theories other than seizure of capital goods, private properties, collectivization, and slave labor camps.

Their conclusion was that social class conflict was the essence of Communist/Socialist ideology. One hundred years ago, Vladimir Lenin's configuration of socialism was to be a solution for the pernicious class struggle of the peasants, and a way to end the imperialistic Romanov dynasty. Lenin's progressive socialism was in reality a contrived revolt against the social and political order of most European governments. These nihilists openly admitted that their goals could only be accomplished by forceful termination of existing laws and civilities. Their aim was total elimination of private property ownership, abolish all religious worship, and centralized (government) control of all labor, wages, and redistribution of wealth.

Lenin's totalitarian mandate was to successfully abolish entrenched laws and present-day civilities. This included elimination of all private property and religious activities. Establishing strict government controls of communal labor and redistribution of wealth would be accomplished in conjunction with the forceful seizure of government agencies. Lenin did not hesitate to act. All land and contingent properties were confiscated for government use with no recompense for the ravaged victims. A **"decree of Land,"** written by Vladimir Lenin, was approved, passed, and legislated by the Second Congress of Soviets. It was an incorrigible piece of legislation seemingly unenforceable by any government agency. Absurd or not, the **nationalization of private land** in the Soviet Union became a way of life for the next seventy years.

On the heels of confiscation and nationalization of properties, comes the second social re-engineering action: An atheistic attack on the peoples religious beliefs. Denial of all religious worship was viciously enforced in spite of pitiful cries by millions of Orthodox Russian Christians.

The essentials of socialism henceforth were; (1) deprivation of Private Property, (2) desecration of religious worship, (3) progressive socioeconomic programs in which an elitist government controls all methods of production and the proper levels of output and appropriate final pricing. **Unfortunately, such a classless utopian society was never to be.**

"Raison d'etat:" a purely political reason for action on the part of a ruler or government for privileged national goals, while denying basic principles of justice, morality, or the individual rights of people. This clearly defines the crucial tenets of socialism.

"Rule of law:" a true democracy for the people, and by the people, who live and die by the rule of law: a political belief that is in direct conflict with the outlandish "Raison d'etat" of socialism. The principle of democracy affirms that all people and institutions are subject to and accountable to laws that are fairly applied and enforced. Our time-honored rule of law is never to be entirely separated from the people who make up our society.

Herein lies a classic study in contrasts. When a populous nation embraces a secular government that rejects religious moral standards, abolishes eternal truths in contradiction to all past historical experience, and in place of logical relevance substitutes a philosophy of "the ends justify the means," its citizens inevitably become subservient to the rulers state and bear untold consequences. Factually, a societal and economic crisis follows, even worse: self-ordained totalitarian leaders turn into evil agents of enslavement, genocide, and mass murder. The world has witnessed such and recorded over a hundred million human beings who were needlessly sacrificed during the past century in the name of socialistic communism. It became a syllabus of atrocities, not a viable government. It was the epitome of a vile nihilist movement of old.

Human beings were soon deemed expendable for the good of the state. Millions of nameless victims were enslaved and brutally slaughtered, critically sucking the life out of many countries of the world. The greatest and most dominant Marxist/Socialist leaders of the world--- Lenin, Stalin, Mao, in methodical order with homicidal fury and zeal became the greatest mass murderers in the history of mankind. Historians quit counting after 100 million humans lives, all needlessly sacrificed for an illogical, god-forsaken political concept disguised as rational sociological innovation and a modernized economic system for future utopian governments of the world.

The truth is that historically governments were instituted by honorable men giving valid justification for defined commitments of their government. The moral purpose of government is for the protection of individual rights and freedom. **Foremost of the service that government renders is to keep its people alive, and safe. The right to life is the fundamental source of all rights**. Other rights in life, are actions of lesser consequence. Unfortunately too many people fail to grasp this basic concept. Rights are not a gift of society or some government award. The purpose of government law is for the protection of individual rights, and the source of the government's authority is to be: "the consent of the governed."

Their unrelenting charge was an abdication of rationality, denial of religious authority, and deprivation of individual freedoms. The Socialist leaders insisted that morality does not inherently exist and moral values are abstractly contrived. Ever faithful to their **"Catechism of a Revolutionist"**, the new age Socialist-economic movement insisted that passe social and political institutions must be destroyed in order to make way for the new totalitarian state by any means necessary, including terrorism and assassination.

Vladimir Lenin during his last days with Stalin, said, **"First, we will take Eastern Europe, then the masses of Asia; then we will encircle the United States, which will be the last bastion of capitalism. We will not have to attack it. It will fall like overripe fruit into our hands."** Lenin died a year later in 1924. Stalin and Mao Tse-tung kept the torch of totalitarianism lit for a long time, while the United States, a democratic republic, prevailed, and those bastions of capitalism with free enterprise proliferated.

Socialism was and is the backbone of totalitarianism and the soul of a consuming government. Twentieth century communism created a belligerent schism with the rest of mankind, not only due to the abolition of private property, or collectivization, communal living, enslavement, and denial of God and religion. It was the insidious rationale, **"the ends justify the means,"** that ordained genocidal murder of undesirable people. A record massacre of 100,000,000 human beings were sacrificed in vain for the sake of a hypothetical, materialistic socialistic ideology.

Note:
"The Moloch of Totalitarianism"--- A monumental shrine was erected in memory of heinous acts of human sacrifice in Europe.

CHAPTER 11

The Moloch of Totalitarianism

There exists today in Europe a guarded monumental symbol of human evil. Few are aware of the ubiquitous Moloch, holder of tyrannical power perpetuated by subservience and human sacrifice. The spectacular "**Moloch of Totalitarianism**" monument stands towering outside the gates of Levashovo Memorial Cemetery, in St. Petersburg, Russia, the very city where Vladimir Lenin first gained political notoriety back in 1905. The sinister story of Levashovo was a well-kept secret for half a century. During the years of the "Great Communist Terror," prominent totalitarian dictator, Joseph Stalin had tens of thousands of former kulaks, suspected anti-Communists, and various ethnic enemies of the state shot without trial. The politburo of the Central Communist Committee secretly had the slaughtered victims stacked high in government trucks and dumped at the wasteland of Count Levashovskaya for a mass burial. For many years, a dense forest grew over the burial site under the watchful eyes of assigned guards. After the collapse of the Soviet Union, the site of the cemetery was declassified and eventually revealed to the general public. A renowned sculptor, Nina Galitskaya and Vitali Gambarov created and erected the impressive edifice titled "Moloch of Totalitarianism." There also is a multitude of related shrines erected as testimony to the sacrificial acts of inhumanity during the last century. A requiem mass is celebrated at the memorial site annually on October 30, for the faithful attendees. It is their "Day of Remembrance," for the sacrificial victims of Totalitarian Politicos.

CHAPTER 12

The Peninsula of Korea

For a thousand years the Chosen dynasty of Korea kept its society po-litically independent, a culture insulated from other nations until the **"Hermit Kingdom"** *was* annexed by Japan in the summer of 1910. Imperial Japan's unconditional surrender of World War II also ended thirty-five years of enforced colonization of Korea by the Japanese. Korea was liberated in August 1945 only to be denied autonomy as a country. In the aftermath of the war, the Korean Peninsula was parti-tioned at the 38th parallel as negotiated by Stalin (Yalta Conference) at a Russian resort in the Crimea several weeks before US President Franklin Roosevelt's sudden death.

North Korea was immediately overrun and ruled by Communist Soviet troops. The southern half of Korea was occupied and sup-ported by American troops. The South Korean government opted for free market Capitalism under the democratic leadership of Syngman Rhee. By Communist design, a similar divisive scheme was acqui-esced to the Soviets which in effect divided East Germany into a strict Communistic society as opposed to the Free Market Democratic so-ciety of Western Germany. Conflict in Korea was inevitable. Stalin would never allow free elections anywhere, only one party of secular, socialistic Communism.

By 1948 Stalin withdrew his Soviet troops from Korea, leaving behind a cadre of military, weaponry, and Soviet advisers under the leadership of Kim Il Sung, a legendary Communist guerrilla hero. True to Stalinist Communist ideology, Kim Il Sung in turn nationalized the economy, confiscated property, collectivized land and civil liberties, and imposed a ridged totalitarian system, including the use of slave labor camps in remote locations near the borders of Russia and China. Often entire Korean families, including children, were incarcerated for "guilt by association," and then all were sentenced without trial and imprisoned for three future generations in order to permanently wipe out the seeds of evil. Thousands upon thousands of North Koreans labored, starved, and died young. It was treasonous for anyone to ever leave the country; few ever escaped. Kim Il Sung built up a large army intent on utilizing his ideology towards a reunited Korea. In 1950, ten thousand North Korean troops sanctioned by Stalin and, led by Kim Il Sung, crossed the 38th parallel to launch a war with the South Koreans. **The Korean War was** a civil war that became **the first instance of open warfare that pitted communism against a capitalistic society.**

North of the Yalu River lies the border of China. It was there where yet another Communist civil war raged on for dictatorial control of China. Mao Tse-tung's Communist horde of guerrilla warriors routed Chiang Kai-shek's retreating Nationalist Army clear off mainland China onto the Island of Formosa (Taiwan) in the South China Sea. The victorious Mao Tse-tung, hailed as China's reigning Communist conqueror, was a celebrated guest of honor at Stalin's seventieth birthday in Moscow where they conferred and soon after signed a joint Sino-Soviet Friendship Treaty. All of China ultimately capitulated to Communist forces. Stalin made haste to convince Korea's Kim Il Sung to meet with and confide in Mao as fellow guerrilla warriors. He advised Kim Il, that Mao like him, was a committed Communist with a thorough understanding of all Oriental matters and best of all, Mao had at his command at least three hundred thousand seasoned troops, which could be utilized in the battle for Korea. This could be a shared interest for any future global confrontations with the United States or any of the United Nations.

Mao Tse-tung agreed to back Stalin and Kim Il Sung. He entered the Korean War as the grandiose savior of fellow Communists but was careful not to officially mention of declaration a war. Instead he chose to lead Chinese combat divisions under the guise of being "peoples volunteers," ready to fight belligerent South Koreans and their allied American troops. Mao covertly dispatched 250,000 Chinese troops across the Yalu River in the dark of night to attack their new enemy. Stalin offered to provide air support for Chinese combatants with Soviet MiG-15 fighter jets. "MiG Alley" became the renowned birth-place of new jet airplanes engaged in aerial dogfights. Within two months, North Korea's army greatly reinforced with hordes of Mao's Communist troops succeeded in reversing the direction of the battle, but the onslaught only intensified the onslaught and prolonged the war.

The ferocity of the Chinese Communist attack left stacks of dead warriors littering the battlefields mixed-in with thousands more of critically wounded from both camps of battle. Adding to the pathos was the collateral: the massacre of innocent children, women, and the aged, caught in the path of war often outnumbering military casualties. The total dead, wounded, and missing amounted to over four million victims of endless bombing, and bitter winter weather, with no heat, shelter, food, or medicine. They were left to forage under a heinous scorched-earth policy set by the enemy.

In 1953, after three brutal years, the carnage peaked in June and by July's end, the killing stopped. Unexpectedly, talks of armistice were discussed and signed by North Korean and Chinese communist commanders. The USA signed for the other side but, South Korea refused to sign the armistice without reunification.

The cease fire by communist North Korea was unforeseen. Coincidental to their change in military attitude, Premier Joseph Stalin suffered a massive stroke that instantly killed him. It seems that it was indeed Stalin's war and the new Soviet leadership had enough and put a provisional stop to the war. Bemoaned were the violent practitioners of Lenin's communistic precepts and Sergei Nechayev's "Catechism for Revolutionists." A eulogy was in order for veneration of Joseph Stalin, unfortunately his legacy was that of systematic genocide, being the **"mass murderer of 30 million"** of his own people and adherent of: "the ends justify the means."

The politically divided Peninsula of Korea remains a historical vestige of tragic injustice. The small Hermit Kingdom was cast into a politically charged civil war by outsiders, triggering the slaughter of millions of forsaken people who resisted a Communist ideology that achieved nothing but suffering and death. By 1953, five million armed soldiers had successfully killed each other, and yet it remained a rare bloody war without an end. There never was a formal declared armistice and six decades later there still is no mutually signed peace treaty. After all these years, North Korea stands primed for military combat, wary of non-Communist countries, while its people remain poor and half starved in a politically depleted economy.

In stark contrast, after the cease-fire, South Korea chose the Western path of a capitalistic, free-market republic with a democratically elected president. They South Koreans voted for and utilized an export industrialization strategy to produce labor-intensive products. They engaged in programs of privation to minimize the role of government in the economy. South Korea rose up from the ash bin of war in one of the poorest corners of earth; to become a dynamic society that is ranked thirteenth largest economy in the world. No longer a recipient of foreign aid, South Korea today is a major contributor to foreign aid for other countries, which ironically includes the still hostile Communist country of North Korea.

Be that as it may, the dreaded "domino effect" of totalitarian communism plays on in Asia much to the distress of the free world. "There is no substitute for victory," said; General Douglas MacArthur, Supreme Commander of American and United Nations forces in Korea at the time. **"The Communist threat is a global one. You cannot appease or otherwise surrender to Communism in Asia without simultaneously undermining our efforts to halt it in Europe."**

CHAPTER 13

Maoism

The First Five-Year Plan took effect in 1953 for the Communist People's Republic of China. Its leaders leaped into the Soviets' totalitarian form of government all for greater economic activity and agricultural expansion of their vast landscape. Although Joseph Stalin was dead, Mao Tse-tung lived on in the mold of Stalin, an equally case-hardened Communist leader with little regard for human life. Mao's disdain for the dignity of mankind was unmistakable when, like Stalin, he too mandated the nationalization of business and collectivization of all agriculture, properties, tools, animals, and farmland before forcibly herding unsuspecting masses of humanity into designated government communes. Then, with great expectations and pride, Chairman Mao Tse-tung heralded it as the, **"Great Leap Forward."**

By 1956 all banks were nationalized. No longer was there a privately owned company in China. Collective farming produced oppressive farming methods and squalid food distribution systems that resulted in worst famine in human history. Chairman Mao had created a model totalitarian-Communist state and, with Stalin dead, claimed to be the greatest Communist in the world. In the meantime starvation engulfed all of China. Within three short years, thirty million Chinese people starved to death.

His horrendous scourge did not halt here. It evolved into a rampant political paradigm of annihilation. Mao Tse-tung declared that intellectuals were social misfits to be dealt with and did so by proclamation, this time under the label of the **"Great Cultural Revolution."** He tried to justify his inhumane governance by rationalizing that there was a time when "Emperor Huang of the China dynasty" found it necessary to bury alive only 460 scholars. "We have buried alive forty-six thousand scholars." Mao further bragged that gangs of loyal young Communist's roamed China's villages, and city streets, targeting enemies of the state or anyone determined to be a reactionary, especially writers and teachers. They were always to be physically humiliated and often beaten to death. The purge of intellectuals was carried out and ceased only after another million Chinese were sent to their graves.

As Marxist mentors before him, Mao also promised utopia but instead instituted programs of genocide. He likewise constructed forced labor camps throughout China. For nearly thirty years, fifty million subjugated Chinese toiled in Mao's version of the Soviet gulags. Twenty million ravaged inmates died after laboring for years in primeval camps all for the sole promulgation of Maoism. The Chinese economy may have stagnated since the sixteenth century but it took Mao's Totalitarian socioeconomic programs, "Great Leap Forward" and "Great Cultural Revolution" to turn China into one of the poorest countries in the world.

Historians estimate that sixty million Chinese people died under Mao's totalitarian trial of communism in the most populated country on earth. In spite of forced famines, inhumane imprisonment, and being the mass murderer of the century, never-the-less, millions of Mao Tse-tung celebrants ignored his life cycle of inhumanity. Mao in the end was deified; his writings ironically remain revered scripture. The exalted spirit of the first chairman of the Chinese Communist Party lives on.

Portrait of Mao / Photo, c.1960
akg-images / IMAGNO/Votava

Upon Mao's death the Communist Party of China faced a power struggle between left-leaning and rightist government officials. "The Gang of Four," an influential group of leftist radicals, were arrested and put on trial. Deng Xiaoping, a rightist came into power. Deng and his allies expelled the Gang of Four and the former cultural revolution with it's failed class-struggle ideology was denounced.

"The Four Modernizations" was the new central theme that marked a significant change in modern Chinese history. The Communist Party tilted right to free-market oriented reforms starting with agriculture. Collective farm communes ceased, and plots of land were granted which became the responsibility of private property owners. Next, private business ownership was permitted, and the rise of private entrepreneurs was a first for socialistic Maoism. A revised dual pricing system above and beyond central government constraints was a major step that made profits a new criterion. When China's privatized industry was given freedom to compete with other major markets and economies of the world, using capitalistic formatting, there was voluminous growth and profits, all of which remains a work in progress.

CHAPTER 14

Polish Solidarity

During the summer of 1980, an unexpected labor strike erupted at the Vladimir Lenin Shipyards in the port city of Gdansk, Poland. After decades of Communist rule by the tyrannical Soviet Union, no one anticipated that a gang of besieged Polish workers, let alone the entire eastern block of Europe, would ever take the first steps toward freedom. It all started when a hundred shipyard workers demanded that Anna Walentynowicz, a day worker and a factory electrician named Lech Walesa be reinstated. They both had been unjustly dismissed for organizing an independent trade union. Workers protested that they all were underpaid, overworked and sick and tired of living under a communist lie. The entire Polish community sympathized with the mistreated shipyard workers.

The protest gained momentum and turned political, as an outright emblematic social uprising. What emerged was a non-violent movement that was rallied on by work groups in the cities of Gdansk and Warsaw, Poland. Within days Lech Walesa was reinstated. He found his way back to the shipyards with the help of fellow workers. They followed his lead by organizing a larger Regional Inter-Enterprise Strike Committee, and defiantly elected their hero, Lech Walesa, as chairman.

The labor movement, being non-violent, gained the attention of the Catholic Primate of Poland. Cardinal Wojtyla, along with sixty prominent intellectuals published a societal letter of criticism citing twenty-one humane postulates. They demanded basic human rights of justice and equality, freedom of speech, printing and publishing, release of political prisoners, strike rights, and access to mass media for people of religious faith. The Eminent Cardinal Wojtyla in the mean-time was elevated by the Vatican in Rome to pontiff of the Catholic Church. As Pope John Paul II, he conducted open-air masses in vacant fields, preaching to his flock of millions about, "human rights and not to be afraid... seek out your freedom of livelihood." The phenomenon of "solidarity" by this time included not only Poland but other European countries that were driven to resist totalitarian domination.

Communists officials were not about to give in or surrender to any sort of Polish resistance. Arrest of the orderly, nonviolent protesters were made by the thousands. Their behavior only aroused greater wrath from the Soviets but sympathetic approval from Western Europe and America. The unmitigated movement was branded **"Solidarity,"** and the protester's motto became **"For our freedom and yours"**. The flame of freedom ignited all of Europe, and the march to freedom became unstoppable. This first non-Communist union in the USSR soared to over nine million citizens. Massive movements of people were determined to put an end to living and working under the dictates of totalitarian rulers.

Enraged Soviet leaders were swift to impose aggressive martial laws. Russian armored tanks in close columns rolled up and down the city streets in an attempt to crush the people's defiant stance, but in the end, the Soviet military commanders ultimately were ordered to stand down and negotiate a peaceful resolution with none other than the voice and leader of "Solidarity," Mr. Lech Walesa. His legendary accomplishments merited him a Noble Peace Prize, and soon after, he became the residing president of Poland. The flame of liberty burned brighter across Europe and the path to freedom was visible.

Mikhail Gorbachev, general secretary of the Communist Party by 1989, gave a public address that the USSR would no longer interfere in the internal affairs of Eastern Europe. **The Union of Soviet Socialist Countries fell into severe economic decline and in desperate need of social and economic restructuring.** The events that began in Poland prevailed in Hungary, East Germany, Bulgaria, Czechoslovakia, and Romania. Romania was the only country of the group to experience violence before defeating the Communist regime. A hated Romanian dictator, Nicola Ceausescu and his wife Elena were executed by a firing squad in central Romania. Soon after Albania, and Yugoslavia also abandoned the USSR.

After four decades of suffering through Marxism, Lenin, and Stalin's heinous Socialist tyranny, a requiem clarion tolled the demise of the totalitarian USSR. The entire Soviet block of countries began to collapse like dominoes, one by one. Fifteen new nations avowed independence and freedom, leaving Russia to stand alone and broken. The free world remained fixated with one eye on the decline of the Union of Soviet Socialist Republics and one eye on the "Berlin Wall."

CHAPTER 15

The Berlin Wall

The **"Berlin Wall"** was a worldwide symbol of tyranny, the dichotomy of evil and good. At the end of the Second World War, the territory surrounding Berlin was controlled by Russia. A division of Germany was agreed upon at the Potsdam Conference. West Germany was to be the zone of occupation for American and Allied forces, while East Germany would be under the jurisdiction of Russia. The capital city of Berlin, though technically part of the Soviet zone, was split with West Berlin being occupied and controlled by American and Allied forces.

West Germany elected to become a democracy, and their free-market economy soon prospered. Meanwhile East Germany, a Communist state deteriorated into a zone of oppressive poverty. German citizens began to flee in mass. A thousand a day of skilled laborers, professionals and intellectuals, all fled Communist East Berlin, for the prosperous American zone in West Germany.

By 1948 the Russians in anger blocked all the roads and railroads leading into West Berlin. This cut off all food water, and medical supplies; starvation was eminent. The Soviet's also vehemently rejected any economic assistance or available aid from the American Marshall Plan. They would not tolerate any outside aid for their former enemy

(Germany), which had almost devastated them. The Soviet leaders militant stance made it crystal clear that Stalin intended to isolate Eastern Europe from the West and implement his totalitarian doctrines across the continent. Joseph Stalin had managed to survive a series of wars and now planned to continue with conquests over penetrable territories with his own firebrand of communism.

There was a method to his madness. "Divide et Impera," said, Julius Caesar. The way to seize and maintain political power is **"Divide and Conquer."** Caesar's tenant was Stalin's dogma. He used it to an extreme and seized absolute control within the Communist party. "Divide and conquer" was again enforced in Asia, precisely at the 38th parallel of Korea. Stalin blocked any political elections in North Korea, and then took aggressive action against the democratic Republic of South Korea. Once again in Europe, Stalin utilized the city of Berlin to separate and blockade East Germans in the Soviet Communist Zone. Entrapped, the East Germans were forced to live and work as dutiful Socialists under the eyes of Russian border guards, well isolated from the contagious high-life witnessed in West Berlin's democratic zone.

The Russian blockade intensified into a major international conflict for American and Allied Forces stationed in Berlin. Withdrawal from the city was clearly not a viable option; all of Europe would be at the risk of caving into a totalitarian government, just like Stalin's Union of Socialist Republics.

A coordinated airlift of food for the starving was determined to be the best counteraction. Without forewarning, American and British cargo planes loaded with food and medicine dropped out of the clouds, flying dangerously low over the Berlin blockade, while Russian soldiers stared skyward at the incriminating show of strength by the damned Allies. The massive airlift of food and medical supplies was a success. East Germans were provided with enough food and supplies to live comfortably on a continuing basis. After eleven unstoppable months of Allied airlifts, the blockade became a Russian nightmare that continued to confound their status. The blockade was discreetly called off by the politburo in Moscow.

This proved to be an important victory. West Germany became a beacon of democracy and freedom in what was otherwise called *a cold-war fight against communism*. By 1961 exodus of East Germans peaked at three million emigrants. The dwindling population threatened the feasibility of a sustainable communist state in East Berlin. Stalin was enraged; he considered eastern Germany his spoil of war to do with as he pleased. Russian agents were freed to seize East German equipment and ship valuable properties back to Moscow for distribution.

It was a hot August evening in Berlin, and the whine of power saws and jackhammers broke the silence of the night. The commotion was the work of Russian laborers erecting a grotesque twelve-foot brick wall trimmed with razor-sharp barbed wire and a gun tower for military guards. If that wasn't sinister enough, a crew returned later and built a second wall separated from the first by 160 unobstructed yards, creating a **"death strip"** of floodlights, trip wires, and 300 armed guards with orders to shoot-to-kill. In the dreadful days that followed, a barrier of a million land mines was placed between East and West Germany. These horrific structures along the 850-mile border separated East Berliners from families, friends, and available jobs in West Berlin. The Berlin Wall clearly delineated the irreconcilable concept of totalitarian governance. East Germany was a solidly socialistic Communist state, ruled by Soviet Russians, while West Germany, under American jurisdiction, depicted a classic study of contrasts. One of free markets, capitalism, and all-embracing private ownership sustained by a thriving economy in the Republic of Germany… **just beyond the shadow of the Berlin Wall.**

Soviet bureaucrats had the nerve to claim that the wall was built purely as a security measure to protect liberated Germans from ex-Nazi terrorists. It also was to set an example of the Soviet Union, a superpower transforming Communist East Germany into a showcase of the moral, political, and economic excellence of a socialist government, rather than the debauched capitalistic trial going on in West Germany. The truth was that the wall never was protection from outside dangers but in reality was, an extreme measure by a cruel totalitarian government determined to keep freedom-loving people from trying to escape to the West. Some of the entrapped did get away, but unfortunately hundreds of other East Germans died trying to escape either over, under, or through the hated "Berlin Wall."

Pity those poor souls being quelled by a casual glance over their high, barbed-wire wall, just to see the glow of city lights and hear the resonance of night-life on the western horizon. Gun towers or not, **too many of the do-or-die desperate risked it all to escape the condemnation of communism, on the slim chance of reaching the shelter of freedom in the West German zone of democracy.**

Germany's once proud capital city remained divided, isolated, and impoverished for four decades. The inhumanity was carried on right to the very end in 1989. The last of the East Germans to scale the wall, landed in the **"death strip"** *w*here he died in a hail of bullets. It should be noted that, no one from the West was ever shot trying to get into East Germany. Among the successful escapees over the years were disillusioned border guards. It became common practice for the guards to run for it, when no one was looking, Much to the chagrin of the Russian Politburo, a total of six hundred of their own guards escaped over the years. They too chose to live among all those freedom-loving capitalists in the democratic zone.

In November 1989, thousands of East and West German protesters stormed the Berlin Wall. The surging horde managed to tear down a broad section of the concrete wall. West Germans forced their way through the opening in the wall while passive border guards watched other screaming East Germans jump for joy just west of the wall. In one week, nine million East Germans charged westward seeking jobs, better living conditions, and political freedom. The Berlin Wall at last was ritually smashed to pieces by thousands of skeptics until it's final removal.

The Fall of the Berlin Wall / Photo, 11th November 1989
akg-images / picture-alliance / dpa

West Germany which flourished as a capitalist society, had experienced such rapid economic growth that it was christened the "Economic Miracle of the Rhine." The Soviet Union's totalitarian plenary trial of communism in East Germany, on the other hand, proved to be the antithesis of the economic miracle enjoyed in West Germany.

Thirteen months after the collapse of the Berlin Wall on Christmas Day 1991, Mikhail Gorbachev resigned from his office as president of the USSR and the Communist monolith, the Union of Soviet Socialist Republics was dissolved and Eastern Europe was reborn. **The Union of Soviet Socialist Republics was dissolved and Eastern Europe was reborn and renamed.**

CHAPTER 16

French Indochina

The French established the **East India Company** to create trade and commercial business in the Orient. By 1668 they established a foothold in the territory. Over the ensuing, years France gradually gained formal control of three colonies: Cambodia, Vietnam, and Laos. Emperors were removed before the French assumed power in 1887 and renamed the colonies **"French Indochina."** In 1925, a little more than five thousand French leaders ruled thirty million Indonesians. The French were justly proud of their modernizing programs, creating paved roads, electric networks, modern medicine, schools of higher learning and a humane justice system but not all the people were thrilled with their new French styled civilization. The French met with armed resistance by some defiant Vietnamese. There were Marxist revolutionaries among the protesters: the belligerents were called the **Indochinese Communist Party.**

During the 1930's, the French struggled to keep Indochina in check. When World War II broke out in 1941, Japanese troops charged ashore and took over Indochina while Germany defeated France. World War II came to an end in 1945. Japan was defeated and, under the terms of an unconditional surrender, had to relinquish all conquests, including Indochina. The French being liberated victors, returned to reclaim their beloved French Indochina but were challenged by a coalition of Communist Vietnamese jungle warriors.

The leader of the Vietnamese Communists was a native, well educated in France and fluent in French, Chinese, Russian, and English languages. Ho Chi Minh ("bringer of light") was a world traveler; it was while living in Paris in 1920 that he first joined the French Communist Party. He was so inspired by Vladimir Lenin's Bolshevik revolution that he left Paris to study more about the revolution in Russia. While in Moscow, Ho Chi Minh learned well the Leninist techniques of agitation and propaganda, so well that the Comintern Congress in Moscow sent him on a mission to organize a revolutionary movement in China. However Chinese officials were not ready for his methods; he was charged with inciting anti-government Communist activities. Ho Chi Minh returned to Moscow and waited for three years before being sent back to Canton, China. This time he served as a special advisory to Mao Tse-tung's Chinese Nationalist Army.

Ho Chi Minh, a trailblazer of North Vietnam, and commander of the Viet Minh Guerrilla forces, proved to be a formidable adversary of the French Occupation Forces in Indochina. He was a pragmatic Communist. A doer more than theorist in the land of Confucian virtue. Ho was an intelligent man, small in stature, and of fragile health, yet he was very dedicated and capable and nonetheless cunning and ruthless. His strength lied in the devotion of nineteen million Vietnam natives, along with armed guerrilla force of thirty thousand jungle fighters much to the distress of the French Legionnaires. Ho Chi Minh in his youth was a seafarer who matured into a cunning world traveler with the intellect and disposition of a seasoned diplomat.

Ho Chi Min / Photo
akg-images

Deep in the heart of a jungle in Northern Vietnam was the isolated headquarters of Ho Chi Minh. It was from this remote location, that he coordinated a massive military force called the **Viet Minh's.** He did it all with peerless tact, carefully maintaining a balance of control between the Soviet Union and Chinese National Army. He had an ulterior motive: to get more weapons, artillery, and military advisers. The United States military stationed in South Vietnam grew increasingly alarmed. It was a matter of critical strategic importance for them to contain any further Communist uprisings in southeastern China.

It was inevitable that war would break out between Ho Chi Minh's hostile guerrilla forces and the French troops occupying Vietnam. The imminent conflict worried Congress and President Eisenhower who publicly warned that this could possibly be the start of a **"domino effect."** This military theory governed American foreign policy at the time. President Eisenhower feared that if Vietnam fell under Communist control, it could very well affect all of Southeast Asia.

A Communist victory in one nation might result in a chain reaction leading to the downfall of neighboring nations. In the wake of World War II, the United States sought lasting peace not that, *"the fear that many human beings pass under a dictatorship. that is inimical to the free world."*

In the beginning, French troops launched a fierce attack deep into North Vietnam, leaving a bloody trail of casualties. Most of Ho Chi Minh's forces eventually slipped past the French, back into the dense jungle. The fighting turned into thorny jungle warfare. The French were at a distinct disadvantage and suffered mounting casualties. The War for Indochina escalated greatly after Mao Tse-tung was victorious over Chiang Kai-shek, leader of the Republic of China. In 1950, Communist China and Stalin's Soviet Union formally recognize their ally Ho Chi Minh and his new Democratic Republic of Vietnam (Communist) government. China and Russia in turn send military advisers and automatic weapons. The armaments kept coming; mortars, howitzers, trucks, ammunition and the guerrilla force was transformed into five conventional army units and one heavy armored division.

After eight years of jungle warfare the battle-weary French retreated to the high ground of a small mountain outpost near the border of Laos. The French army hunkered down at their fort and air field in the valley of **Dien Bien Phu,** never suspecting that the lofty peaks above the valley could possibly shelter forty thousand troops of Ho Chi Minh's army or that in the caves of the mountainside were heavy artillery weapons with Chinese gunners. It was the rainy season; the end was near when two hundred howitzers loaded with new Russian Katyusha rockets opened fire with the sound and fury of all hell pounding down the mountain on the hapless French encampment and airfield. The French Foreign Legion was decisively crushed: ten thousand survivors laid down their weapons, raised their arms and surrendered. It marked the bitter end of the French rule in Southeast Asia. Regrettably for the free world, the first of the theoretical domino's was about to fall. Ho Chi Minh's Communist forces were victorious, but only in North Vietnam, up to the 17th parallel. The Republic of South Vietnam remained defiantly anti-Communist. Nearby Laos and Cambodia were independent neutral countries, but peace was doubtful with an emergent **Laotian Communist Party.**

This first Communist war in Vietnam (French Indochina) resulted in seventy-five thousand dead Frenchmen, sixty-four thousand wounded, and forty thousand captured. Vietnamese fatalities were much worse with three hundred thousand dead combatants and the collateral killing of one hundred fifty thousand civilians. The mortality rate was astronomical when one considers, at this point the killing had stopped for the time being. Vietnam was successfully **divided** in half at the 17th parallel but not yet conquered**,** and Ho Chi Minh remained resolute not to be denied his ultimate goal: a reunited--- all Communist Vietnam.

CHAPTER 17

Cambodia

Saloth Sar was an obscure, soft-spoken, young man living alone in France when he decided to abandon his college studies in favor of returning to his homeland. Saloth had recently joined a progressive Communist cell in Paris. Soon after, he set off on a life-altering mission. He was no longer a bored, struggling student but a born-again social reformer, obsessed with the idea of launching a political revolution of his own making.

Saloth's birthplace was a sleepy little fishing village in French-Indo china when he was last there. To his disbelief, it changed considerably and was now called an independent state of Cambodia. Once back home he assumed a peculiar lifestyle of seclusion and mysterious behavior. Saloth Sar played the role of a bookish country gentleman, charismatic and was well liked by his neighbors. His career and daytime activities were outwardly that of a mild-mannered, private school teacher of the French language, along with history, geography, and a civics.

But at night--- his psyche tripped into a dual personality the likes of Dr. Jekyll and Mr. Hyde. In the dark of night, he was the fearful leader of a band of black hooded genocidal terrorists; only they knew that Saloth Sar was none other than the notorious **Pol Pot**, the ruthless demagogue of the extreme **Communist Party of Kampuchea, or "Khmer Rouge".**

By 1970, Pol Pot commanded a revolutionary Communist Party of three thousand armed killers who beset a genocidal reign of terror on Cambodia. His Khmer Rogue group was peerless, not to be mistaken for other Communist groups in Vietnam. Pol Pot's objective was to purify and rebuild his own special agrarian society by molding everybody into energetic, rural farm hands. Cities, he claimed were nothing but evil cabals; all cities had to be ransacked and purged for productive workers in his new world of agricultural communes. Individualism was passe; instead radical morals, spirited collectivism, and discipline would be the new way of life. Pol Pot's fanatical scheme included elderly men and women, the blind, sick, and lame, even infants. All were to be removed from the evil capitalistic cities and put to work in collective farming groups.

The time had arrived in 1975 for another Communist domino to fall: North and South Cambodia. The Khmer Rouge army swelled to seventy thousand well-disciplined military troops. Pot Pol unleashed a cold-blooded, broad-based purge of all native Cambodians. Being another paranoiac Communist leader, Pol pot's mode of operation was to maintain a curtain of secrecy, authoritarian discipline, and absolute terror. His Khmer Rouge forces were programmed in Communist tactics, armed with Russian AK-47 rifles, and given marching orders to empty the cities, burn the villages, and haul the survivors to countryside slave labor camps. Pol Pot's unyielding passion was to create a purely totalitarian agrarian state, devoid of any social institutions, such as banks, libraries, churches, schools, and manufacturing plants. He, as others before him, totally abolished religion, ownership of private property, and he only permitted state-approved marriages. The Khmer Rouge, avowed **"This would be the first nation to create a completely Communist society without wasting time on intermediate steps."**

Intellectuals, businessmen, upper-class people, and foreign ethnic groups were executed on sight. Thousands were promptly and purposely sacrificed in order to change the country from a self-serving modern society to an anesthetized agrarian society of progressive Communists. The slaughter went on…teachers, students, Buddhist monks, cripples, the insane, sick, and weak. Covert programs of genocide required mass graves to be dug by fellow Cambodians. The magnitude of gross carnage was exposed and classified by the media as, **"The Killing Fields of Khmer Rouge."**

Pol Pot distinguished himself, as one of many totalitarian tyrants who ruthlessly dismantled and destroyed an entire country, leaving in his wake two million slaughtered Cambodians…all for a delusional political program offering Utopia; that in reality ended up in "the killing fields."

The Khmer Rouge army made a critical mistake by starting a border battle with Ho Chi Minh's Viet Cong guerrilla forces. Enraged Vietnamese troops mounted a vicious counterattack upon the tunneled Khmer Rouge troops, causing Pol Pot to retreat deep into his jungle fortress. The elusive one never got captured, so his enemies found him guilty anyway and sentenced him to death. Undaunted, Pol continued to direct guerrilla battles against the Vietnamese or any other enemies.

He lived out his remaining years in the foreboding jungle of Cambodia. The psychotic dictator, now much older and wiser, and bordering on death, conceded to a candid personal interview. The rendezvous point was a clearing deep in the jungle. A jaundiced Pol Pot woefully stared across a wooden table, and divulged to a reporter,* that he wished his life's work could be undone. Then passively he states, **"When I die, my only wish is that Cambodia remains Cambodia and belongs to the West. It is over for Communism, and I want to stress that."**

*Nate Thayer * Washington Post*

CHAPTER 18

The Vietnam War

The French Indochina War ended at the **Battle of Dien Bien Phu** after eight years of jungle warfare. It was a mortifying defeat for the French government. France took pride in its hundred years of colonial rule in Vietnam, Cambodia, and Laos in Southeast Asia. It was a devastating defeat, and Paris had no recourse but to surrender and assure immediate withdrawal of all living French forces.

Ho Chi Minh, a charismatic leader of the revolt, abandoned his remote jungle command post for new headquarters in Hanoi. From there he continued to command the Viet Cong military forces up to the 17th parallel where a temporary battle-line **divided** the North from South Vietnam. The North was strengthened by the Soviet Union (USSR) and Mao Tse-tung's People's Republic of China. South Vietnam's military and village nationalists remained staunch anti-Communist combatants who had the backing of the United States military and other anti-Communist allies. It was an explosive state of affairs that gave rise to an ongoing buildup of military troops on both sides.

The primary goal of United States was to create an independent non-Communist government, south of the 17th parallel, and to provide Vietnamese nationalists an option other than another totalitarian government pursued by the Union of Soviet Socialist Republics. It was necessary to summon an international assembly to secure an ongoing peace in Vietnam. The **Geneva Accords Conference of 1954** was critically important with grave consequences possible if the situation was not suitably solved by the international policy-makers adjourned in Geneva, Switzerland.

Operation Passage to Freedom was their recommended agreement; it authorized three hundred days of open borders allowing the Vietnamese people to relocate in North or South Vietnam depending on their preferences. An unbelievable surge of **one million Vietnamese fled from Communist North Vietnam**. They voted with their feet, and their catch phrase was **"God has gone south!"** Seventy-five percent of the population was Christian; the other 25 percent of the migrants were non-Communist property owners. All fled North Vietnam for repulsive political reasons. Christians escaped religious persecution, while all endured seizure of their private land and properties by a totalitarian regime.

Ho Chi Minh early on established a solid base for his totalitarian government. North Vietnam was already a totally Communist state ruled by one party soon to be governed by a Soviet style politburo. After duping unwary peasants, Ho launched a sweeping "**program of land reform**" following the familiar model (collectivization) of other Communist nations. Private and public land was confiscated, homes were seized and ransacked. North Vietnamese landowners were hauled before "people tribunals" and tens of thousands were executed or sent to forced labor camps. The confiscated land and property was then utilized by the government for communal living quarters and agriculture. It became a period of ideological cleansing and death--- in all a half-million people perished. Ho Chi Minh's absolute power had changed Vietnam into a hostile country of carnage.

Nine countries convened for the historic Geneva Accords of 1954 hoping to secure peace in Vietnam; instead it turned into an acrimonious event. China assumed it was a major player at the round table while their duplicitous partners, the Soviets, challenged all suggested ways and means for a peaceful coexistence. Other members of the assembly took issue with a dubious coincidence between Vietnam, the Peninsula of Korea, and Berlin, Germany. Each contested the conclaves of communism as created by the Soviet Union and Mao's China: and how after being violently divided were methodically subjugated one by one. Ho Chi Minh's preached his hollow message of unity and tolerance while his minions were busy confiscating private land and, properties and slaughtering Christians in North Vietnam.

Unfortunately the disparate policymakers failed to resolve any crucial matters other than an accord for a temporary "passage to freedom," which was realized only after the US Navy humanely agreed to expedite the mass exodus to South Vietnam. A final declaration for local elections never got scheduled and the 17th parallel division remained the boundary line. The Communist leaders finagled appeasement concessions that served their own national interests. Western countries under strict orders for containment not warfare, remain nonaligned. Rational peace negotiations stalled, discord prevailed, and subsequent agreements went unsigned by all parties. **The French government was quick to announce its total withdrawal from Southeast Asia. The United States elected to stay on and did so for twenty more blood-filled years.**

The temporary truce was soon ignored when the Viet Cong attacked strategic targets in South Vietnam. The Viet Cong equipped with heavy weapons continued to attack villages, even American military installations. The United States brought in an additional ten thousand military advisers. Ho Chi Minh's forces stepped up the conflict when two patrol boats opened fire on navy destroyers. The US Congress in turn authorized a military increase for the region and 200,000 American combat troops arrived in Vietnam.

Ho Chi Minh declared war and proclaimed that all of Vietnam, North and South, would be under his governance. He dispatched Viet Cong forces for an all-out attack in South Vietnam with, an ultimatum to make Vietnam one unified Communist nation. Their rebellious neighbor Laos joined with Vietnam, also in pursuit of a new form of government. The **Lao People's Revolutionary Party was made up of** organized anarchists of Laos, who were also seasoned jungle warriors; they too chose to fight and die under the banner of communistic nationalism right alongside the Viet Cong.

US President Lyndon B. Johnson announced that he **"will not lose Vietnam"** and then dispatched another thirty five hundred marines to defend South Vietnam. The battle intensified with a two-stage bombing of military installations over North Vietnam and Laos. Operation Rolling Thunder (one hundred bombers) continuously dropped bombs for three years. US Navy warships patrolled the waters of the Gulf of Ton-kin while thousands of Chinese troops remained camped along the border. The death of the aging Communist potentate, Ho Chi Minh, changed nothing. The longest war of the twentieth century raged on as the unyielding Viet Cong held their ground.

A river of Russian military aid flowed into the jungle wilds of North Vietnam, including modern ground-to-air missiles and; anti-aircraft guns, along with Soviet combat training classes for Viet Cong gunners and pilots. Vietnamese piloted, Russian made MiG-17 and MiG-21 fighter jets turned the tide of war.

What started as guerrilla warfare vaulted into a full-scale land, sea, and air war. After nine long years of saturated bombing and thousands of devastating air attacks, the U S Air Force by now had over a thousand aircraft shot down with many lost pilots, yet the war continued on endlessly. The number of American combat troops involved peaked at over 540,000 before the bitter end… ten years later.

The Communist regime had once again methodically set out to divide and conquer the self-governing people of a neighboring country and they succeeded. In the long run, the appalling cost was: Allied military dead 282,000, Communist military Dead 444,000, Vietnamese civilians dead… 587,000.   **Total Dead… 1,313,000**

Be it the Korean Peninsula, the Berlin Wall, a city in Cambodia, or the jungles of Vietnam, all were victims of "**political cognitive dissonance,**" regarding societies with incongruous political ideologies and attitudes by the opposing states. If ones devotion to the cause was so powerful, as was the case with past totalitarian dictators, **"the ends justify the means."** There was no sane resolution.

The Vietnam War also known as the Second Indochina War came to an end. Once again, there was no military victory for the dead or those missing in action, **a**nd alas still no real peace even though a cease fire agreement was signed by all. The South Vietnamese were to abide by new Communist edicts. The American soldiers and diplomats were withdrawn by 1973. Life was not the same under the Communist Party. It became unbearable…no religion, no freedom, private property confiscated and people chased out of their homes. The South Vietnamese bravely fought on unaided until suffering final defeat in 1975. In the end, South Vietnam alone had sixty thousand people killed and a million more sent to prison for reeducation or incarceration.

A historic tide of **"boat people"** defied the new Communist law and fled their homeland via the South China Sea. Under the cover of night, they would slip away in small rickety boats that were jam packed, often with a hundred refugees in small quarters. Many poor souls drowned at sea, or were killed by Thai pirates. Nevertheless, throngs followed, and soon tens of thousands of "boat people," including natives of Laos and Cambodia. **The tidal wave of boat people escaping communism was endless for the next twenty-five years. It created a**

political and humanitarian conundrum for the international community. A majority of the refugees resettled in America. By the end of the century, over two million Vietnamese had left the country of their birth to restart new lives in foreign lands.

Aftermath:

Ho Chi Minh's explicit control of the Vietnamese faltered. The country never developed a viable economy under his totalitarian government. The socialist plan for collectivist agriculture failed to produce enough food to feed the people and private property rights were denied. It became one of the poorest nations in the world. Living conditions continued to deteriorated until late in the century, when nationwide reform programs were petitioned. Political changes were enacted: decentralization of farm land and approval of private property ownership uplifted the economy. Further reformist of agriculture, along with freedom to buy, sell and trade commodities improved living in the countryside and immediately reduced the poverty level. The new century guaranteed greater capitalism when the stock market was launched in Vietnam on July, 2000. The boom of the stock market and real estate speculation in Vietnam gave birth to a little tiger economy in Southeast Asia.

Conclusion

Western thought, man's faith in human progress and facility to create a world of justice and peace, was rooted in Greek philosophy, Roman law, and Christianity. In the course of civilization, philosophical and social science terms were relativity static until the ideological wars of the twentieth century.

A new age concept of totalitarian governance denied individualism and ordained a credo of collectivism and terror, with action plans well suited for any crazed power-monger ready and willing to try. Socialistic, anti-religious, communal ideologies armed aspirant totalitarians with infinite power over issues of state and all facets of society. Many resolute secular tyrants did implement their own Marxist-Leninist classless socialism and with inane brutality. **The macabre reality was that; empires virtually collapsed from war, famine, and pestilence, with a death toll of no less than 100 million human beings…the very essence of apocalypse.**

Twentieth century totalitarian trials recorded numerous historic atrocities that dehumanized mankind and virtually upset the balance of worldly progress. Perhaps it was critiqued best by Sir Winston Churchill during his address to the House of Commons:

"Many forms of government have been tried in this world of sin and woe. No one pretends that democracy is perfect or all wise. Indeed,

it has been said that democracy is the worst form of government, except all those other forms that have been tried from time to time... Socialism is a philosophy of failure, the creed of ignorance, and gospel of envy. The inherent vice of capitalism is the unequal sharing of blessings. The inherent virtue of Socialism is the sharing of misery."

The United States of America remained a republic, whereby the supreme power was vested in the people and exercised by them through a system of representation via periodic free elections. The American political philosophy was clearly delineated in the second paragraph of the U.S. Declaration of Independence:

We hold these truths to be self-evident, that all men are created equal, that they are endowed by their Creator with certain unalienable Rights, that among these are Life, Liberty, and the pursuit of Happiness--- That to secure these rights, Governments are instituted among Men, deriving their just powers from the consent of the governed,--That whenever any Form of Government becomes destructive to these ends, it is the Right of the People to alter or to abolish it, and to institute new Government, laying its foundation on such principles, and organizing its powers in such form, as to them shall seem most likely to effect their Safety and Happiness. (July 4, 1776)

"America will never be destroyed from the outside, if we falter and lose our freedoms, it will be because we destroyed ourselves."
Abraham Lincoln

Democracy and totalitarianism are prevailing systems of government in today's world. The totalitarian governments of Russia and Eastern Europe eventually collapsed and then changed to more modern economical systems. With it the engine of prosperity coursed over the recovering environs with positive results.

Meanwhile, anti-capitalist, socialistic programs continue to undermine fledgling governments of Venezuela, Argentina, Brazil, and Cuba, as well as vast territories of Africa and Asia. The pity of it all. History is rife with failed totalitarian socioeconomic entities as well as numerous case studies of convoluted political ideologies.

Socialism is the nucleus of totalitarianism that drives the phenomenon of an all consuming government. It is perpetuated by an insidious dogma in which the ends justify the means and communal property, enslavement, genocide, and the diabolic inhumanity of man killing man are embraced. All for the sake of a god forsaken materialistic ideology.

The basis of democracy is liberty and limited self government. These freedoms encourage individualism and greatly improves the quality of life. Perpetuation of the state comes with a cost, that of constant vigilance against unwanted totalitarianism. Regrettably, democracy is assailable and can be compromised during periods of crisis, then woefully regress into a polity of inhumanity. Some say the roots of mans humanity, and even his inhumanity, are inherent with the political community. Rational citizens and legislators must admonish irrational political concepts via the ballot box whenever individual freedoms are denied for reasons of greater government control. Remember well that it was a regrettable system of government that gave rise to a variety of power-lusting dictators during the twentieth century. That was a cruel century in which the ends justified the means, including horrific genocide. Tyrannical leaders seized upon the offering of new socialistic criteria and the militant governance of a totalitarian government. We the people must realize and renounce all matters suggesting, collectivism, nationalization of business, progressive taxation, open borders, abolition of private property, and the denial of religious worship. They are not to be bartered at the cost of our long-abiding unalienable rights of life, liberty, and the pursuit of happiness. Confirm the sanctity of life, the dignity of man, the rule of law, and moral ethics. Honor and respect all that is hallowed in our republic and always keep it …. **one nation under God, with liberty and justice for all.**

Wherefore what's past is prologue.

What to come, is in yours and my discharge.

William Shakespeare

www.ingramcontent.com/pod-product-compliance
Lightning Source LLC
Chambersburg PA
CBHW072327290526
45794CB00002B/768